Gunay Bagirova

Linguistic personality in artistic discourse

Gunay Bagirova

Linguistic personality in artistic discourse

Linguocultural aspect

ScienciaScripts

Imprint
Any brand names and product names mentioned in this book are subject to trademark, brand or patent protection and are trademarks or registered trademarks of their respective holders. The use of brand names, product names, common names, trade names, product descriptions etc. even without a particular marking in this work is in no way to be construed to mean that such names may be regarded as unrestricted in respect of trademark and brand protection legislation and could thus be used by anyone.

Cover image: www.ingimage.com

This book is a translation from the original published under ISBN 978-3-330-32018-5.

Publisher:
Sciencia Scripts
is a trademark of
Dodo Books Indian Ocean Ltd. and OmniScriptum S.R.L publishing group

120 High Road, East Finchley, London, N2 9ED, United Kingdom
Str. Armeneasca 28/1, office 1, Chisinau MD-2012, Republic of Moldova, Europe
Printed at: see last page
ISBN: 978-620-7-51802-9

TABLE OF CONTENTS

1. THE PROBLEM OF LINGUISTIC PERSONALITY IN MODERN LINGUISTICS

"Linguistic personality" represents one of the most relevant concepts of modern linguistics. It is clear that this concept should not be perceived by itself, in isolation from the peculiar semantic field created by the anthropocentric paradigm. Each of the fundamental concepts of modern linguistics is often perceived as absolute. This manifests the evaluation of both the concept itself and the reality behind it.

In our opinion, the very term *linguistic personality* may well be regarded as tautological. Human personality manifests itself in language. In the same way, peoples leave their memory in writing. In the history of culture, it is customary to distinguish between written and pre-written periods. Writing itself is oriented at preserving speech and language. In this connection, it would be appropriate to recall M. Heidegger. Usually linguists, when referring to the German philosopher, repeat the common phrase that he called language nothing but the *house of being*. In M. Heidegger's fundamental work "Being and Time" there is, in our opinion, a more important for us reasoning about language. M.Heidegger writes: "Man sees himself as a being that speaks" (21, p. 165).

M. Heidegger operates with ancient Greek conceptions of man and shows that calling man a rational animal is a later fact, since for the Greeks man was first of all a speaking animal. He writes: "Is it a coincidence that the Greeks, whose everyday existentialism invested itself primarily in speaking-animal-to-friend and who at the same time "had eyes" to see, in the pre-philosophical as well as in the philosophical interpretation of presence defined the being of man as ζῷον λόγον ἔχον. The later interpretation of this definition of man in the sense of animal rationale, 'rational living being,' is true not 'false,' but it conceals the phenomenal ground from which this definition of presence is derived" (21, p. 165).

Thus, the reasonableness of a person is associated with his speaking. M. Heidegger does not specifically stipulate, but it is clear that the speaking person speaks in society. The speaking person in this function is formed by society, so the speaking person is a social person.

The term *socialization is* widely used in modern linguistics, philosophy, cultural studies and even foreign language teaching methodology. The meaning of this term is transparent, and socialization means becoming a full-fledged member of society. The real content of this complex process is revealed, apparently, by the spheres of human activity. A person, being formed as a member of society, adapts to its norms. These norms cover all spheres of life activity, and, of course, the most important place among them is occupied by language as a means of communication. Looking ahead, we can note the role of student jargon or jargon in general in the formation of a person as a full-fledged member of society. Jargon often pursues corporate goals, it is an indicator that this individual is *his own*. In a student group, those who own the jargon are a special corporation. It is commonly thought that student jargon is focused on expressive designation of old and well-known concepts. In fact, student jargon quite clearly fulfills the conspiratorial function. Those who possess the jargon sufficiently form a kind of elite group. Other members of the student community feel like outcasts, as their communication with representatives of the elite group is incomplete.

A student group is a kind of a cell of society, full-fledged joining it is an aspect of socialization. In a broad sense, socialization means an individual's accession to the values of society. In the first place in the process of culturalization of a person is mastering the language of this society. V.V.Krasnykh writes: "Socialization is the process of a child's ingrowth into civilization; the main process during which a child assimilates (appropriates) the experience accumulated by previous generations; in the process of socialization an individual becomes a person, a person speaking, a member of a certain national-linguistic-cultural community" (11, p. 160).

The meaning of the term *socialization*, as noted above, is largely determined by the internal form. It is really about the formation of a social individual. However, it is also impossible to absolutize the social beginning in this case. An individual assimilates not only social norms, but also concepts significant for his native culture. Strictly speaking, in this case we are dealing not with socialization and not so much with socialization as with conceptualization of consciousness. Of course, even in this case we can say that both the language itself and its conceptual side are not individual, but social. Consequently, the process of language acquisition itself is also social in nature. And yet, just as speech is individual in nature, the conceptualization of consciousness is also individual in nature. Besides, in the process of conceptualization of consciousness the spiritual potential, which, as Y.S. Stepanov puts it, is not verbalized, but only experienced, plays a great role. In general and in general, such acquisition of cultural values can encompass a variety of private phenomena. For example, it is believed that culture is united around a fundamental text. In this case, personal identification is oriented towards this kind of fundamental text. For example, Arab consciousness was formed around the Koran. A. Schimmel, a researcher of Muslim mysticism speaks about even Quranization of the memory of Muslim mystics (23, pp. 38-44). Russians still believe that not only the modern Russian literary language is the language of A.S. Pushkin, but also the consciousness of the people is formed by Pushkin's spirituality.

The experience of the last decades unambiguously shows that language personality types (hence language collectives) are still being formed today. Apparently, this process always remains incomplete. It is quite fair to correlate the formation of linguistic personality with the differentiation of language into spheres of activity. If language is a social phenomenon, serving the needs of the human collective, then the differentiation of spheres of activity leads to the differentiation of language. Such differentiation is both logical and consistent. In his time D.E.Rosenthal pointed out: "Language as a social phenomenon performs various functions related to this or that sphere of human activity. The most important social functions of language - communication, message and impact. For the realization of these functions historically formed and formed separate varieties of language" (16, p. 18).

Therefore, the very definition of *functional* in the term *style* is legitimate. Moreover, the functional character of a language is inherent in its embryo, which directly programs its differentiation. In other words, a natural language cannot but differentiate itself functionally, since the very notion of "function" presupposes further development. Since natural language phylogenetically and functionally develops as a social phenomenon, its differences are determined extra-linguistically.

Based on this, it can be argued that spheres of activity represent a dynamic social system, simultaneously stable and variable. This does not call into question the existence of such stable functional styles as official business, scientific or journalistic, but is programmed to form more and more new corporate languages or peculiar argos. In our opinion, all these styles and argos represent a single system, in the structure of which functional styles constitute the socially significant core, and professional and corporate argos - the periphery. For example, in the last two decades the computer business has acquired a special significance in the life of society. Everyone, from small to large, uses computers, but there are few specialists in this field, programmers and masters. At the same time, it is characteristic that computer specialists began to organize themselves into a kind of caste, allowing themselves even a somewhat disdainful attitude to the rest of humanity. O.I. Ermakova, who is specially engaged in this issue, points out: "The community of "computer users" is a rather closed social group, isolated from the rest of society, but the closed nature of this group is not conspiratorial (as, for example, in thieves' jargon), but is a kind of "collective game". At the same time, the peculiarities of jargon language use (peculiar "rules of the game") are always a certain sign of belonging to this group, a signal that distinguishes between one's own and strangers" (8, p. 247). Thus, the fundamental distinguishing feature of any corporation - another language - is emphasized once again.

No matter how distant the prerequisites for differentiating between different groups and society as a whole may seem, mastering such a peculiar jargon as the language of computer scientists also constitutes socialization. In other words, the individual becomes socialized in language.

Academician V.V.Vinogradov can be considered the founder of the theory of linguistic personality in Russian-language linguistic discourse with good reason. In fact, already in his fundamental "Essays on the History of the Russian Literary Language of the XVII-XIX Centuries", as well as in

"The History of the Russian Literary Language" V.V.Vinogradov lays the foundations of the theory of literary language. Separate problems of the formation of linguistic personality are touched upon by him in such works as "Materials and researches in the field of historical lexicology of the Russian literary language", "Word and meaning as a subject of historical-lexicological study", "Notes on the lexicon of the "Life of Savva the Sanctified" and others. V.V.Vinogradov considers the history of the formation of the national Russian literary language in the context of the formation of Russian culture as a whole. The history of the formation of the Russian linguistic personality is thus analyzed against the background of the formation of the norms of the national Russian literary language. Thus, in V.V. Vinogradov's works the theory of literary language is in close contact with the history of the formation of Russian culture and, perhaps most importantly, with the history of the formation of Russian man.

A.S. Pushkin is a model of linguistic personality for Russian culture. In our opinion, we can trace the formation of linguistic personality on the example of this outstanding representative of Russian culture. Of course, not every even intelligent person of Pushkin's epoch could correspond to Pushkin's type of linguistic personality, nevertheless A.S. Pushkin embodied the main tendencies of development of Russian man as a linguistic personality.

A.S. Pushkin was characterized primarily by a pragmatic attitude to language. He proceeded from what best fit into the text and thus contributed to the achievement of maximum communicative effect. In A.S. Pushkin's language, perhaps more than in any other, the main criterion for the selection of linguistic means was communicative efficiency.

The communicative effectiveness of speech is an understandable requirement, which in principle does not require any special explanations. Nevertheless, it is worth dwelling on two points. Firstly, it is quite appropriate in this connection to touch upon the issue of behavioral characteristics of speech in general. Secondly, the problem of communicative effectiveness of speech acquires special relevance from the point of view of poetic speech and, in general, the activity of a poet or writer and his role in the history not only of literary language, but also of national language in general. In this connection, it is not superfluous to recall the fact that the Russian literary language is still called Pushkin's language.

Behavioral characteristic of speech can take place exclusively on the background and in the aspect of communicative effectiveness. Nowadays, no one doubts the idea that speech is an activity. Sometimes one speaks of language in action. Whatever the process of speaking is called, it is quite unambiguously oriented towards achieving a certain goal. The thesis that speech is an activity means, first of all, that it is goal-oriented, goal-directed.

Speech as an activity has its addressee in mind. Consequently, the meaning of speech and its functional significance is determined only by whether the goal pursued is achieved or not. This task is solved by each individual precisely as ζῷον λόγον ἔχον, since any individual realizes his human givenness not only by formal speaking, but by speaking aimed at achieving the goal. In this aspect Pushkin was simply a man whose speech gave him certain advantages over others. Such advantages were also possessed by other representatives of the epoch, who knew how to "achieve their own ends by speech". It should be clear that the linguistic personality realized itself to the maximum extent in certain spheres of social activity. For example, the ability to speak and get one's own way is especially prominent in the speech of lawyers. It is equally important for teachers. Consequently, linguistic personality manifests itself in the ability to achieve explicitly set or implicit goals. That is why this characteristic of a speaking individual is behavioral.

The problem of communicative effectiveness of speech becomes extremely important also from the point of view of the history of literary language, in particular, poetic language. The nature of the phenomenon is the same - we are talking about a linguistic personality that has a powerful influence on the formation of other linguistic personalities. Such influence can be both directly-individual and indirectly-literary. Thus, Pushkin had a great influence on the fate of the Russian national literary language. This is the reason for today's feeling of direct living connection of the poet's language with the language of the people, which makes Russian people call the modern Russian language the language of Pushkin.

High designations of the activity of the great Russian poet have become in principle a commonplace phenomenon, but few people know what is the essence of that transformation in the sphere of language, which obliges us to call the Russian literary language the language of Pushkin.

The linguistic personality created by Pushkin's genius has historically been, first of all, the bearer of cultural tradition. Sometimes, when evaluating the poet's activity to transform the literary norm, one recalls only its innovative side. Meanwhile, any outstanding representative of culture is first of all a bearer of traditional values. If Pushkin only opened access to common words and expressions in the language of fiction and limited himself to this, his language would be deprived of literary roots. If he had limited himself to the wide introduction of Gallicisms, it would have been a mere epigonism to Western models. The language would have subsequently gotten rid of both. It is known that national literary languages are nourished by the life-giving juices of the living colloquial language of the common people.

The influence of individual features of an outstanding linguistic personality has a decisive impact on the formation of mass linguistic consciousness in all epochs, but in the period of intensive formation of norms of the national literary language it acquires special importance. The fact is that the absence of normative dictionaries and reference books naturally leads to the orientation to the language of great writers. If today what is correct is what is fixed in reference books on literary norms, then in Pushkin's and later epoch what was correct was what Pushkin had. If Admiral Shishkov and other purists considered it their duty to fight Pushkin's innovations, the speaking and writing masses followed Pushkin's patterns because it was beautiful and, therefore, effective from the communicative point of view.

Y.N. Karaulov devoted a special study to the phenomenon of linguistic personality. It is significant that in his book "Russian Language and Linguistic Personality" he speaks about the historical perspective of the formation of the idea of linguistic personality as a central idea in linguistics. Y.N.Karaulov defines four paradigms in the history of linguistics: historical, social, psychological and system-structural. The term *paradigm* itself, of course, is used in the sense in which it is interpreted by T. Kuhn in his book "The Structure of Scientific Revolutions", but there is some redeployment of concepts. Thus, in the history of linguistics it is customary to define three paradigms, considering the first one to be comparative-historical. The goals, methods and principles, meta-language and understanding of the nature of both the object (language) and the subject (linguist) constitute our idea of a paradigm. It is generally accepted that the comparative-historical paradigm has ceded primacy to the system-structural paradigm. At the end of the 20th century, cognitive linguistics became more and more widespread.

Y.N. Karaulov defines paradigms taking into account the dominance of general ideas about the object. Thus, he cites G. Paul's words that language is historical through and through (10, p. 12) and says that the sense of language historicity was dominant in the 19th century, hence, it is possible to define the historical paradigm. At the beginning of the 20th century, interest in the psychology of language intensified, thus the psychological paradigm was formed. F. de Saussure defined such theses as "language is thoroughly systemic" and "thoroughly social", hence, the systemic and social paradigms in linguistics are defined (10, p. 14). As we can see, we are talking about the priority of ideas or even the aggravation of interest in one or another aspect of language, aneo paradigmality in the sense defined by T. Kuhn.

It is characteristic that Y.N. Karaulov sees the human factor in the formation of all four paradigms. It is hard not to agree with this, since it is a peculiar attribute of man. It is interesting that in this connection he polemizes with F. de Saussure and writes: "Paradoxically, but it is a fact: no linguist nowadays will sympathetically quote Saussure's idea that the only object of linguistics is language considered in itself and for itself" (10, p. 19). As it is known, when preparing the Course of General Linguistics for publication, Sh. Bally and A. Seshet introduced a lot of things into the text of the notes they used that were not there. As A.A.Kholodovich points out: "Now all these shortcomings of the course recreated by Bally and Seshe became even more obvious after the critical edition of the Course was published in 1967-1968" (19, p. 20). It is known that the final phrase of the Course belongs to the publishers, not to Saussure. At the same time, Y.N. Karaulov's remark corresponds to the logic of his reasoning. Thus, he notes that, despite disagreement with Sossiur (albeit falsely interpreted), many linguists subconsciously proceed from this thesis. He writes: "Due to the general inhumanity of the modern linguistic paradigm, the place of the truly anthropic factor in it, the place of the anthropic character of the language image it creates is taken by the anthropomorphic, human-like one, generated by the desire to liken - to animate, revitalize, humanize - the dead image" (10, p. 20). The scientist considers various language stamps of linguists and comes to the idea that language is mythologized in linguistic discourse.

As Y.N. Karaulov himself notes, in the process of formation of this or that paradigm, as a rule, the aspect of analysis that constitutes the center of research interests is hypostasized. At the same time, none of these aspects has the ability to unite them all: "As a result, the normal consideration of one of the properties inevitably looks like hypostasizing" (10, p. 21).

Thus, the analysis of the properties of linguistic personality allows us to establish its historical and cultural character. Linguistic personality is formed in the process of socialization. As for socialization, in most cases it is presented as an acquisition of cultural tradition.

2. LINGUOCULTURAL PROBLEMATICS OF THE ARTISTIC TEXT

Linguoculturology is formed and intensively developed at the end of the last and beginning of the present century. The anthropocentric paradigm is the impetus for the development of linguoculturology.

The terminology involved speaks for itself at the level of internal form. Thus, the term *anthropocentrism* has a transparent structure and in principle is reduced to the semantics of the immediate components. The term implies that in the center of scientific research is a person with his spirituality, attitude to the world, peculiarities of perception and rethinking of information coming from external sources.

The central concept of the discourse under consideration is the concept of "culture". The word *culture* itself is one of the most widely used in all languages. This peculiarity is purely linguistic in nature, but it is caused by extralinguistic factors, i.e. factors external to the language. The main reason for this phenomenon is, in our opinion, that man is a product not only of nature, but also of culture, and it is important that the culture that shapes him is created by him.

The "World Encyclopedia. Philosophy" defines *culture* as it is understood today, noting its essential features. Thus, it is indicated: "CULTURE (Latin cultura - cultivation, upbringing, education) is a system of historically developing suprabiological programs of human activity, behavior and communication, acting as a condition for reproduction and change of social life in all its main manifestations. The programs of activity, behavior and communication, constituting the corpus of culture, are represented by a variety of different forms: knowledge, skills, norms and ideals, patterns of activity and behavior, ideas and hypotheses, beliefs, social goals and value orientations, etc. In their totality and dynamics they form historically accumulated social experience. Culture stores, broadcasts (transmits from generation to generation) and generates programs of activity, behavior and communication of people" (6, p. 524).

The Encyclopedic Dictionary notes the most essential features of culture, covering both material and spiritual phenomena. It refers to the facts of social, political, economic, educational and other spheres of activity. In principle, culture includes everything created by man. It is important that "culture stores, transmits and generates programs of activity, behavior and communication of people". The role of language is implicitly represented in this statement. Moreover, everything said is directly related to language, accumulated through linguistic mediation and realized in the same way. It turns out that the statement or assertion that "culture stores, transmits and generates programs of people's activity, behavior and communication" has an essential presupposition. The informational essence of this presupposition consists in designating the sphere of language functioning, its socio-historical significance, although this phenomenon is never named.

If culture stores, it stores first of all information, which is encoded in language. If a culture transmits programs of behavior, it transmits them in the form of language. If it generates, it generates them in the form of signs. Thus, outside the field of linguistic coding a culture can neither store, nor transmit, nor generate its values.

It should be noted that the term *culture* in this case is a kind of metonymy. By culture it is necessary to understand a human carrier of culture, cultural values. The socialization of a personality in principle is nothing but the acquisition of the world of culture and the world of language, which in the process of personality formation are completely inseparable and indistinguishable. It is this factor that causes a naive view of the world, which can also be called philistine, when the meaning of a name is associated and, moreover, identified with a thing.

A cultural personality, a carrier of culture, not only reproduces culture, not only transmits it, but also transforms it. Thus, the cultural personality is not a passive reproducer, slavishly following the existing norms.

Acquaintance to the norms of culture can be identified with socialization, but in any case the framework of culture represents a certain procrustean bed for the individual. When a person finds himself in certain rigid conditions of existence determined by culture, whether native or foreign, he is forced to obey them. Otherwise he risks becoming an outcast. Culture is a good thing, but its history is replete with protest based on the rejection of norms. As V.M. Rozin notes, "new generations of people are connected to culture, and as a result of the functioning of culture, new situations and ruptures arise, it rethinks traditional ideas, and mechanisms of translation, adaptation and innovation are formed" (17, p. 208).

In our opinion, the mechanism of stabilization of innovations in the space of culture is very similar to the models of scientific revolutions described in his time by the American scientist Thomas Kuhn. Throughout his book, Kuhn gives many examples that show that in the history of scientific knowledge, new knowledge is always perceived as absurd at first. As the new knowledge becomes established, the old knowledge, which recently seemed unshakable, begins to be perceived as absurd.

The main working thesis of linguoculturology can be defined as follows: "Culture is represented in texts. The text represents the encoded content". Consequently, the culture of a people can be studied only through texts. On the other hand, it is impossible to study language without cultural content. In this case, the text is understood in the broadest sense. A text is a single word, hence, a phraseology, a proverb, and a proverb. Behind each of the linguistic texts there is a huge content. It is necessary to distinguish between background information and conceptual content. Background information in principle is not limited culturally and culturally, especially when it comes to fundamental phenomena of life. Therefore, native speakers perceive the same phenomena in different ways, with different degrees of intensity of meaning, because different amounts of background information are involved.

Background information is concretized in space and time. It is broken down into perception of cultural phenomena and reflection about them, which is why it can be labeled as cultural and culturological information.

The content of a concept unites native speakers at the conceptual level. Of course, native speakers as a unified collective represent some abstraction. This is usually manifested in the level of perception of the surrounding reality. This abstraction is concretized by various socio-political and historical-cultural groups. Even native culture is perceived differently by intellectuals and representatives of physical labor. On the other hand, representatives of the same linguistic group may differ in the character of perception of social facts and history. For example, in Soviet times, dissident literature was evaluated differently by different circles of intellectuals. By the way, the word dissident itself means "dissident". The essence of the phenomenon itself is that the dissident's views diverge from the generally accepted and widespread views. In other words, dissidents are always a minority. Thus, the nature of the actual background information distinguishes quite clearly between different representatives of the same people or language group.

However, it should be taken into account that such a difference in the demand for background information does not divide the speakers of a language so deeply that they cease to be one people. And to be one people means, first of all, to have a common world picture. As noted above, the world picture characterizes the whole national collective only because it has a linguistic-ethnic character. For this reason, this phenomenon is most often called not just a picture of the *world* characterizing the mentality of this or that nation, but a *linguistic picture of the world.*

The linguistic picture of the world is *linguistic* because it acquires its ontological status in language. Language unites speakers of one language at a very deep subconscious level. Compared to this deep conceptual level, which unites the nation, all background differences look superficial. Consequently, the system of essential associations represented in the world picture is iconic in nature. This means that not every native speaker is obliged to reflect on the conceptual content of the signs he/she uses. The very operation with the same signs unites the national collective.

Reflections on the content of linguoculturology suggest that there is very little absolutely new in it that has not been stated in cultural history. What is new, apparently, is the sharpened focus on cultural issues. Indeed, it is hard to surprise anyone with the idea that language reflects the psychology and thinking of the people, their culture, ancient beliefs and religion, mythology and environment. In our opinion, the study of the world's languages has always been accompanied by the study of culture, understanding culture in the broadest sense. Perhaps the only exception in this sense is strict structuralism, which saw its task in the maximum formalization of research.

Traditional linguistics has always had linguodidactic goals in mind in one way or another. The study of languages presupposed their teaching. The search for universal languages and the creation of universal grammars was oriented towards teaching them as effectively as possible. What we would call today a country studies or linguo-country studies approach was also derived from the goals of teaching. Thus, in medieval Europe, the study of the languages of the world was given great importance. The cultural and historical significance of monasteries for many centuries was connected with the goals of spreading Christianity. In Christian countries, missionary programs have historically shaped the type of polyglot monk. It was this strategic task that stimulated the parallel study of the life and manners of those peoples among whom Christianity was preached. It was impossible to communicate with peoples without knowing their languages. Knowledge of languages necessarily led to familiarity with culture. Thus, the study of languages has always been accompanied by the study of peoples, their national characters, living conditions and the impact of these conditions on their psyche. Moreover, the mere knowledge of a language was formal. Language was studied not in itself, but as a way of getting closer to the people and influencing them. Consequently, language turned out to be only a means in these conditions. The main aim was to study the mentality of the people to be converted.

Oriental science was also not an exception in this respect. Thus, the famous "Divoni-lugat-at-turk" by Mahmud Kashgari contains a huge amount of ethnographic data. For example, V.A.Zvegintsev writes: "The work of Mahmud al-Kashgari is a real Turkic encyclopedia, which is based on comparativeness as a conscious scientific principle. It is an exceptional comparative grammar and lexicology of Turkic languages in the full sense of the word, accompanied by abundant data on history, folklore, mythology and ethnography of Turkic peoples" (7, p. 19). As is known, Mahmud Kashgari's dictionary contains a lot of texts that are analyzed in the linguocultural aspect.

Thus, it is not necessary to say that the problem of linguoculturology is new for linguistics. What is new is, on the one hand, the approach to the study of language as a whole, the very focus of attention, abstraction from some linguistic facts and concentration on others. On the other hand, the reduction of the goals of linguistics to the study of text. Finally, the third important aspect of linguoculturology is related to the fact that the text is studied in terms of the representation of national culture in it, and above all, of course, spiritual culture.

3. THE SIGN IN THE SPACE OF CULTURE. LINGUOCULTURAL ANALYSIS OF THE TEXT

At present, the problems of language and culture are in the center of attention of linguists all over the world. Linguists working in various fields of linguistics are increasingly coming to the conclusion that language stands between man and the culture he has created. It is a kind of mediator, realizing the real interaction of man with the world around him. Moreover, language connects man not only with the world of culture, the world of artifacts created by him, but also with the world of nature in the broadest sense of the latter. In other words, man's ideas about himself, his own spirituality, as well as the animal and plant world, landscape, physical and cosmic phenomena - everything is reflected in language. Language signs in the broadest sense - words, word combinations, phraseological units, proverbs, sayings, complex word complexes, texts - carry the most important information about the world. The system of this kind of information, fixed in the consciousness of the speaking group, constitutes the linguistic picture of the world, characteristic of this people. Today, very often in the speech of people of various professions, as well as the most ordinary speakers of the language, the expression national mentality is encountered. It is customary to talk about the mentality of certain peoples, understanding it as national character, habits and standards of behavior, values. Often the national mentality is associated with negative or positive features of the people, our stable ideas about them. It is believed, for example, that the national mentality of Germans is determined by their pedantry and love of order, Americans - by entrepreneurship, Russians - by slackness, Turks - by vigor and active life position. Thus, the whole world is reflected in language and only by language we can judge what this world is like in the minds of this or that nation. Linguoculturology as one of the new fields of linguistic research is based on the fact that only through language we can judge both the psychology of a nation and how it sees the world around it and itself in this world. When speaking about language as a real mediator between a person (nation) and the world, we mean, first of all, texts. And the notion of "text" in this case is quite broad, it includes a wide range of phenomena from individual words to large epic canvases. This understanding of language and its most important functions makes it necessary to study the most important texts in the space of this or that culture in the linguocultural aspect. In this aspect, along with folklore, the texts created by the great masters of the word, representing the mentality of their people, its history and culture in the brightest focus of the artistic word, the system of artistic images, come to the forefront. Let us turn to the linguistic facts. In this article we will analyze fragments from F. S. Fitzgerald's story "A Diamond the Size of the Ritz Hotel".

"St. Midas's School is half an hour from Boston in a Rolls-Pierce motor-car. The actual distance will never be known, for no one, except John T. Unger, had ever arrived there save in a Rolls-Pierce and probably no one ever will again. St. Midas's is the most expensive and the most exclusive boys' preparatory school in the world" (25, p. 6).

Despite the ironic subtext, F. S. Fitzgerald in this case reveals himself as a characteristic linguistic personality. First, like a true American, he plays up the distance to Midas' school. He says that no one can accurately ascertain the length of this distance because no one but John has traveled here, i.e., measured the length of the run.

Secondly, he most frankly mocks the predilection of his compatriots for luxurious and large cars. Thus, he creates the humorous name *Rolls-Pierce*, a kind of contamination of the names of two famous automobile firms *Rolls-Royce* and *Pierce-Arrow*.

Here the writer departs from purely narrative psychology and deliberately ironizes the irresistible passion of his compatriots for everything luxurious. *Rolls- Royce* is a world-famous British car, throughout the last century considered the most luxurious car in the world. The essence of the author's irony is that, according to his belief, Americans are not even satisfied with *Rolls-Royce,* and they prefer to replace it with *Pierce-Arrow*.

In this connection, it is important to emphasize one more point. F. S. Fitzgerald's irony is also purely American in nature; it is the irony of a representative of the aristocracy in relation to the middle class. Not even to the middle class, but to the rich, but to those whom he considers upstarts. These people are rootless to him, they are not descendants of pioneers. This ironic attitude of F. S. Fitzgerald is clearly manifested in his other works. For example, in "The Great Gatsby", "The Night is Tender", "Diamond Mountain". Apparently, this gives reason to argue that F. S. Fitzgerald is an exponent of aristocratic indignation against the dominance of newly rich upstarts. Sometimes such irony is expressed explicitly, sometimes - at the subtextual level, implicitly. But in any case it characterizes the writer as a linguistic personality.

The word *resentment* in this context must be properly interpreted. F. S. Fitzgerald is not just annoyed by rich upstarts. As a descendant of the families that built America, he is concerned about the dominance of upstarts, who by their very existence prevent the creation of the country of which the pioneers dreamed. The linguistic means that the writer uses to create images, unambiguously characterize him as a linguistic personality. It is worth repeating once again that linguistic personality is completely incomprehensible outside of socialization.

Emphasizing the fact that Midas is not just an *expensive* school, but an *extremely*, unusually expensive one, is also full of aristocratic irony. That is, rich provincials would simply not send their children to a merely expensive school.

However, even this is not enough, because along with the *most expensive, it is* noted, as if by accident, that Midas is also an *exclusive school.* In other words, this school is not only extremely expensive, i.e. not every rich man can send his son there, it is also inaccessible, even to the richest. It is a school with a limited enrollment. Consequently, even great wealth does not guarantee mechanical acceptance of a child into the school. The offspring of wealthy families must have some other merit in order to be honored as a student at St. Midas School.

"John's first two years there passed pleasantly. The fathers of all the boys were money-kings, and John spent his summer visiting at fashionable resorts. While he was very fond of all the boys he visited, their fathers struck him as being much of a piece, and in his boyish way he often wondered at their exceeding sameness. When he told them where his home was they would ask jovially, "Pretty hot down there?" and John would muster a faint smile and answer, "It certainly is." His response would have been heartier had they not all made this joke - at best varying it with, "Is it hot enough for you down there?" which he hated just as much" (25, p. 6).

A characteristic detail in this fragment is the mention of the similarity of all fathers. It is interesting that even a child like John is struck by how similar his friends' fathers are to each other. Fitzgerald reduces their similarity in context to a joke that John hated. However, the essence of their sameness, of course, is not just the question of whether they are hot enough down there?

An identical joke likely means that these money grubbers just don't have the smarts for more.

John's response to these adults is also characteristic. He invariably replies with a smile that yes, of course.

The analysis of the story shows that it is up to this point in the discourse that the writer's linguistic personality manifests itself most prominently. Of course, in the further narrative the implicitly oriented analysis is able to reveal the peculiarities characteristic of the author's linguistic personality. However, here the watershed between the demonstration of the author's image and the beginning of the narrative proper seems to pass. Later on, the story unfolds, and other characters, or rather characters themselves, are presented as the linguistic personality.

The analysis carried out in the first subchapter of the second chapter allows us to draw some conclusions. The linguistic personality of the author of the story in these introductory fragments is presented quite convexly, the image of the person on whose behalf the story is narrated is clearly delineated. It should also be noted that there is a distancing between the image of the writer, delineated as a linguistic and cultural person, and the images of the characters as they are presented in these introductory fragments characterizing them. The writer keeps his characters at a distance, and this distance is clearly historical and cultural in nature. The differences, which turn out to be quite significant for the realization of historical-cultural types in the space of a fiction text, have a linguistic content. It is the analysis of the linguistic material that reveals the author's linguistic personality as a representative of the American spiritual elite. When analyzing the author's linguistic personality, the full potential of Western spirituality, which encompasses both the American cultural heritage proper and the Western European one, is in demand. The richness of shades, realized in this spiritual space, presents the author of the narrative as a bearer of global values for Western civilization. Perhaps, on an unconscious archetypal level, he varies from being a representative of Western European culture to being a descendant of American pioneers, the peculiar aristocrats who created this country. The key means for determining the role of the linguistic personality in this case is the writer's explicit or implicit irony.

The analysis of F. S. Fitzgerald's story in the linguocultural aspect allowed us to reveal one more important detail. It consists in the fact that the linguistic personality of Fitzgerald's heroes overlaps with his own linguistic personality. He does not just draw social types in a detached way, but lets them pass through his own linguistic consciousness. In other words, the language of the characters is not an artificially structured code, it is let through the emotional and unconscious perception of the picture of the world. Therefore, both Percy and John are as natural as possible in terms of realizing the speech features of the socio-cultural types they manifest. The linguistic personality of these characters makes it possible to get an idea of the real types of people who were the writer's contemporaries. It is interesting that the fantastic beginning, so characteristic of the story and reflected even in its title, does not affect the plan of realization of the linguistic personality. The story serves in this respect as a document of the epoch.

4. COGNITIVISM IN LANGUAGE SCIENCE AND LANGUAGE PERSONALITY

Cognitivism in linguistics is considered by many scholars as an independent direction. Moreover, the expression *cognitive* linguistics is becoming commonly used. They also often speak about the formation of the third linguistic paradigm after comparativism and structuralism, represented by cognitive linguistics. One way or another, cognitive problems are at the center of attention of modern linguistics. This attitude to the object does not exclude systematicity, but rather even presupposes it. The facts revealed as a result of cognitive-linguistic research also presuppose systematization, because only in this case reliable conclusions about the national mentality and its expression in the national language, i.e. the national-linguistic picture of the world, are possible.

Cognitivism covers all levels of the language system, which is quite natural. Since language is not an elementary system but a system of systems, all global phenomena encompass the whole system. In this aspect, the ancient thesis about the direct connection between sound and meaning sounds in a new way. The comprehension of cognitive models of sound is perhaps the most difficult sphere of anthropocentric linguistics, nevertheless, it is the sphere that can shed light on the essence of language (1; 2; 9).

Cognitivism in the most general meaning of the word means the real connection of linguistic units with the national mentality. This general declarative statement should be confirmed by real linguistic facts every time. The analysis of the literature of the question shows that the range of problems of cognitivism in linguistics is extremely wide. In the 3rd issue of the journal "Voprosy Linguoznaniye" for 2013 a note about the 5th International Conference on *Cognitive Science was* published. (12, c. 141). In this regard, it is necessary to pay attention to two points. First, the conference is devoted to cognitive science, but not to cognitive linguistics, but at the same time, a purely linguistic journal, such as the journal Voprosy Linguoznaniya, gives information about this conference, claiming to have mastered the problems. Secondly, the conference is held within the framework of IACI (Interregional Association of Cognitive Studies). Thus, interdisciplinarity is declared as a principle of cognitive research. Hence, it follows that it is inappropriate to speak about cognitive linguistics; we should keep in mind that there is a cognitive science with its own object and its own subject. Nevertheless, not only monographs, but also textbooks under the title "Cognitive Linguistics" continue to be published.

The main concept that organizes cognitive discourse is the concept of "concept". It should be noted that the notion of "concept" is precisely what distinguishes linguocognitive discourse from the interdisciplinary discourse that presupposes a conversation about an independent cognitive science.

The concept turns out to be indeed the central concept of cognitive linguistics, assuming that it does exist. Moreover, language as a whole has a conceptual character, since the expression of extra-linguistic meaning in language is conceptual in general. Fundamentally important for linguistics, and for cognitive science in general, is the fact that signification as a semiotically relevant moment in the formation of language cannot be imagined outside conceptualization. Semiosis itself is conceptualization. Understanding of this fact actualizes anthropocentric problematics in linguistics. Perhaps, that is why it is legitimate to speak about the formation of an anthropocentric paradigm in linguistics.

The central concept of modern linguistic discourse is the notion of "linguistic personality". At the same time, this concept turns out to be quite complex and ambiguous, since it is realized at the intersection of linguistics and a number of related sciences. Of those fundamental concepts that form unified epistemological models with language, it is necessary to single out such concepts as society and culture. It turns out that these concepts do not just form unified epistemological models, but they alone contribute to the realization of the linguistic factor of personality.

The linguistic personality acts as an identifier of the social personality (10, p. 13). These two concepts are essentially connected, one cannot be imagined without the other. Moreover, the analysis has shown that the linguistic personality identifies itself with society, thus the self-consciousness of the linguistic personality identifies it with a social individual, a social unit.

The most important factor of linguistic personality is socialization (2; 3). As a rule, socialization is understood as a holistic process of an individual's mastering the values of the society in which he or she is formed. It is difficult to call this process natural precisely because socialization is not natural. On the contrary, it is entirely connected with culture, i.e. the world that was created by man. Socialization is directly related to culture, but it is inappropriate to mix these notions. Society is a wholly cultural entity. Human society is perhaps the most important phenomenon that distinguishes the world of culture from the natural world. The linguistic individual actualizes both phenomena. As a result of socialization, an individual becomes a social person. But since language is the binding factor of society, the individual as a social person is also a linguistic person.

Theoretical prerequisites for the study of linguistic personality in the space of an artistic text bring the linguocultural aspect to the forefront. The linguistic personality is most adequately represented in the artistic discourse. This is not accidental. The fact is that it is the artistic discourse that most fully reflects the life of language in all its manifestations. In particular, it finds sociocultural manifestation in the discussions about the legitimacy of singling out such functional style as the style of fiction. As it is known, the opponents of the allocation of the style of fiction put forward the thesis about the globality of the linguistic volume of fiction as the most important argument. In other words, fiction is a discourse about everything. All functional styles, depending on the content of a work of fiction, are naturally reflected in it. Consequently, this discourse is adequate to the described culture itself. Hence the most important conclusion of the study that the linguistic personality of the epoch is most fully represented only in the space of fiction.

In the space of a fiction text, the phenomenon of linguistic personality is most clearly revealed in the language of the writer. In other words, it is the creator of the text that is represented in language as a carrier of certain psychological, social, philosophical-ideological and cultural values. It is important to note that if the characters are constructed both artistically and linguistically, the author at the unconscious level demonstrates himself as a linguistic and cultural personality.

There is a specific relationship between text, life and the individual. The text is a special way of comprehending life. Consequently, the writer (author, storyteller) appears as a phenomenon manifesting a special form of personal existence in language and culture. The analysis of linguistic personality in this case reveals those specific qualities of understanding the world, which actually create linguistic personality as a socio-cultural phenomenon.

It is worth noting another very important point related to the realization of the phenomenon of linguistic personality in a fiction text. Since the character of a fiction text is represented discursively, his speech, being a discourse, has the character of self-understanding and self-understanding. This circumstance is even more convexly represented also in the structure of the linguistic personality of the writer or the author of the text. All these terms in this case imply the person from whom the narrative or story comes. The differences existing between these notions are not eliminated, they are merely neutralized in the context of the analysis. Linguocultural analysis at a deep level reveals the psychic, social and historical-cultural personality that does not just tell something, but is realized in this narrative. That is why such self-realization is unconscious.

The linguistic identities represented in a fiction text are structured consciously and therefore relate to reality indirectly. Nevertheless, they also reflect linguistic and cultural reality. It seems that the linguistic picture of the world has a fragmentary character, and each fragment correlates with a certain type of linguistic personality. The study of linguistic personality on the material of fiction should not just be systematic, it should be typologically oriented. The prospects of this kind of research should be aimed at creating a typology of linguistic personality.

The linguocultural aspect of linguistic personality based on the materials of fiction actually implies a serious analysis of well-known folklore texts. Many mythologemes and archetypes should be reconstructed on the material of oral folklore. Oral folklore should be understood as any text reflecting the picture of the world. This includes riddles, omens, anecdotes, conspiracies, curses, various parables, not to mention proverbs and sayings. In general, it is necessary to understand the reliability of the results of linguocultural analysis of linguistic personality on the artistic material.

5. LINGUISTIC PERSONALITY IN SOCIAL AND MORAL ASPECTS

L. Wittgenstein's "Tractatus Logico-Philosophicus" begins as follows: "l.Die Welt ist allés, was der Fall ist. 1.1. Die Welt ist die Gesamtheit der Tatsachen, nicht der Dinge. 1.11 Die Welt ist durch die Tatsachen bestimmt und dadurch , daß es alle Tatsachen sind. 1.12 Denn, die Gesamtheit der Tatsachen bestimmt, was der Fall ist und auch, was alles nicht der Fall ist. 1.13 Die Tatsachen im logischen Raum sind die Welt" (5, p. 5). These lines set the research program not only for the world but also for language, for "The world is everything that happens. The world is a totality of facts, not objects. The world is defined by facts and by the fact that they are all facts. For the totality of facts determines everything that happens as well as everything that does not happen. The world is facts in logical space" (5, p. 5).

The meaning of the presented strategy is that the attitude to the world is formed as an attitude to an event, not to the world of things. If the event is nothing but an event, then the personality is at the center of the event. The fact is that it is the consciousness of the personality that associates things, and not only the things themselves are (objectively) associated with each other. Thus, a fact must be associated not with a thing as some given, but with an event that binds things into facts. This is why it is significant that the world is everything that happens to be.

The objective existence of man in the world objectively presupposes socialization. It is impossible to be and to be outside socialization. The event of a person in the world means the unfolding of this being in relations with other persons and things. This is what happens to be (was der Fall ist).

Since a human being, communicating with the world and socializing, does nothing but perceive information and give it out, any humanitarian research highlights cognition as an independent phenomenon. *Cognition is* commonly understood as the unity of such processes as perception, representation, and production of information. Although the cognitive model is unified, the nature of cognitive differences is represented only at the level of production. Only in speech is the nature of information perception recognized, as well as the nature of its representation. Therefore, the world we are interested in is also cognized through the speaking person.

Socialization and its character are also directly represented in the individual's speech. Thus, the linguistic personality realizes itself as such on two levels. The first level is the level of collective thinking of an ethnos. The second is the level of manifestation of social and cultural differences. Both levels are of great importance for cognitive analysis. The characterization of linguistic personality in both aspects is of generalizing importance. In the first case, the national mentality is evaluated. In the second, the socio-cultural assessment of the personality is given.

In this short article we analyze a wonderful story by E. Hemingway, "The Short Happiness of Francis Macomber". Of course, the central place in the space of the text is not Macomber at all, but the white hunter Wilson. The writer characterizes the hunter's appearance, but the external features only complement the character's speech, not the other way around. Wilson is all in his speech, and it is not by chance that this speech and consequently the characterization of the character ends with Hamlet's famous speech. Thus, Hamlet's speech and, consequently, his worldview are adequate to Wilson's speech and worldview.

Already the first phrase uttered by Wilson characterizes him. For example: "Will you have lime juice or lemon squash?" Macomber asked. "I'll have a gimlet" Robert Wilson told him" (24, p. 85).

The standard situation presented in this fragment characterizes both Macomber and Wilson. The former uses common designations that serve as names of well-known things. In M. Laurier's translation, "Would you like lemon juice or lemonade? - Macomber asked" (22, p. 389). The second is an expressive designation: "I'll have a gimlet" "I'll have a cocktail," replied Robert Wilson (22, p. 389).

The expressive quality of the word used in the original gives a sense of the translation. In the original, Wilson uses the word *gimlet,* whose basic nominative meaning corresponds to the action "to drill". Hence, *gimlet* is not just a cocktail, but something that drills your gut. For example, *eyes like gimlets* means "piercing or inquisitive gaze". Comparing the original with the translation in this small fragment demonstrates the complete failure of the translation precisely because it uses a neutral substitute. Therefore, it is completely unclear in the translation why Macomber's wife says, "I want a cocktail too. I would like something strong" (22, p. 389).

It is not clear to the Russian reader why a cocktail should be associated with something strong. In the Russian and Russian-speaking person's mind, a cocktail is associated not with alcoholic beverages, but with a milkshake. In other words, the word *cocktail* in no way characterizes Wilson in Russian translation. At the same time, *gimlet is* very meaningful in the original text. Firstly, the internal form "boravchik" is actualized. Secondly, this image characterizes Wilson not only as a lover of strong drinks (not just ordinary alcohol), but also as a lover of thrills. We can say that the image of a strong and tough white hunter is already programmed by this "I'll have a gimlet" at the very beginning of the story.

This strategy continues to evolve from utterance to utterance, eventually structuring Wilson's coherent image. The following sentence is also significant. When Macomber asks how he should pay his servants, he says, "What had I ought to give them?" To which Wilson replies, "A quid would be plenty," Wilson told him. "You don't want to spoil them." (24, c. 85).

Wilson, firstly, uses the simple word *quid*. Secondly, he motivates it with *the* phrase *don't want to spoil them.*

The Russian translation does not stand comparison with the original in terms of expression. The translator substitutes all the means that in one way or another characterize Wilson as a linguistic and social person with completely neutral designations. For example, *quid* becomes quite an official *pound,* and *don't want to spoil them.* The English word *spoil* is more expressive than the usual Russian word *spoil, as it* is associated with "spoilage".

The inconsistency of the translation with the original continues. In the original, Wilson says: "You've got your lion," Robert Wilson said to him, "and a damned fine one too." (24, c. 86). In the translation, "There you have killed a lion," Robert Wilson said to him, "and a damned fine one too" (22, p. 390).

The Russian word *wonderful in* no way reproduces the expression of the English word *damned fine,* which at least means "damn beautiful". English *damn is* not substituted in the translation, since *wonderful* corresponds to *fine,* while *damned is* simply ignored. Thus, by consistently removing the expression of the original, the translator creates a completely different linguistic and social persona, in no way resembling the Wilson created by Hemingway.

Interestingly, in some cases, the translator creates an expressive picture that is not present in the original. For example: "Conversation is going to be so difficult," Margaret said" (24, p. 88). In translation: "Then there will be nothing to talk about at all," Margaret said" (22, p. 391).

In the original, the rather prim and utterly formal "Conversation becomes too complicated" becomes a pithy and relaxed phrase. Macomber responds to this with the line "Don't be silly, Margot," (24, p. 88). Translated, "Don't be silly, Margot" (22, p. 391). Don*'t be silly is* also an order of magnitude more expressive than *don't be silly.*

The expression is intensified in the next sentence. Wilson says: "Women upset," said Wilson to the tall man. "Amounts to nothing. Strain on the nerves and one thing'n another." Translated, "Women's bliss," said Wilson. - It's nothing. Nerves, well, and one thing'n another" (22, p. 391).

Wilson says that "women get upset", Russian *blazhya* completely changes the colloquial situation, because it means "quirk", "duria". Of course, *blazh is* much more expressive than the neutral *upset,* but that's not even the point of the distortion. Wilson doesn't think Margaret's crying is a whammy at all. He realizes that trouble has happened, which is why he says that such trouble upsets women. The word *blasé is* not only stylistically incorrect, but it is also inconsistent semantically. In addition, *blasé* combined with the adjective *feminine* characterizes Wilson's attitude towards women, which is not present in the original.

Both a decrease in the level of expression and its unjustified increase ultimately changes the character of the linguistic personality. Of course, one could say that Wilson's image loses nothing in translation, because it is created by the description of his appearance, his attitude to hunting and to life, and his actions. But this is not entirely true, since only his speech belongs to him. All descriptions belong to the outsider observer.

Let us consider another fragment characterizing Wilson. His thoughts on the Macomber couple's relationship: "So she woke him when she came in, Wilson thought, looking at them both with his flat, cold eyes. Well, why doesn't he keep his wife where she belongs? What does he think I am, a bloody plaster saint?" (24, p. 107).

In the translation the phrase again corresponds to the Russian mentality and for this reason a very subtle stylistic nuance is lost: "So she woke him up when she came back, Wilson thought, looking at both of them with his indifferent, cold eyes. Well, he'd watch his wife better. What does he imagine I am, a saint? He'd watch her better. It's his own fault" (22, p. 409).

The English *bloody plaster saint is* not represented in the Russian translation as an integral semantic and stylistic configuration. In the Russian translation, only *saint* is substituted, which is understandable, since it is important for the Russian mentality that a person can be associated with sainthood. Hence such stable expressions as *I am a saint, I am not an angel*, etc.

The expression *bloody plaster saint* means "*bloody* saint made of clay" or "bloody saint, straight out of clay". In the structure of this expression, all constituents are significant, there is not a single empty one in informational and expressive respect. For example, *saint* creates an association with a person not of this world, *plaster* concretizes, which in this case means "holiness", absence of emotions, passion, i.e. he is not made of clay, but a living person. Finally, *bloody* expresses the degree of expression and reveals Wilson's dissatisfaction with himself. It should have been translated: "Well, I'm not a bloody saint, I'm a living man.

The culmination of Wilson's speech characterization, as noted above, is a fragment from Shakespeare, when the hunter identifies himself with the hero of the great playwright: "That's it," said Wilson. "Worst one can do is kill you. How does it go? Shakespeare. Damned good. See if I can remember. Oh, damned good. Used to quote it to myself at one time. Let's see. 'By my troth, I care not; a man can die but once; we owe God a death and let it go which way it will he that dies this year is quit for the next. Damned fine, eh?" (24, p. 116).

"He who dies this year is spared death next year!" Thus expresses Wilson's credo.

In conclusion, it should be noted that the original and the translation present two linguistic personalities corresponding to the two mentalities of English and Russian. The damage of the translation is found in the removal of the expression of the original. Hemingway's speech

characterizes Wilson not just as a character, but as a man whose profession involves outdoor life and danger. This is his social role. He kills and can be killed. This is what defines his speech and him as a person.

6. LINGUISTIC PERSONALITY IN THE ASPECT OF DISCOURSE ANALYSIS

It is known that the same linguistic phenomenon can be considered in different planes, thus acquiring relevance conditioned by the realities of discursive space. Our ideas about the linguistic personality directly connect it with the established society or its fragment, which in this case has no fundamental difference. It is legitimate to understand a society as any corporately closed group of people. The closedness of a social community finds direct expression in language. In other words, if a corporation is defined at the level of identity of goals and socially significant attitudes, its essential characteristic is speech. It is in this regard it is quite natural to consider the language of characters in a work of fiction. The language of a character is a characterizing means, or a means of additional characterization. In this case, it is believed that the most important characteristic is presented in the character's actions. However, since a work of fiction is a verbal space, the system of verbal means belonging directly to the character, in our opinion, is of primary importance from the point of view of his characterization.

It should be noted that in terms of speech characteristics there is no significant difference between the language of representatives of a certain social group and the language of a character in a work of fiction. Moreover, the language of characters allows typification based on social differentiations.

The socio-cultural differentiation of characters' speech allows us to typify world literature in this respect. The speech characterization of characters presented in world literature is naturally of historical and cultural nature. Despite the huge volume of such work, its expediency is undoubted.

In modern linguistics, the strategy of analyzing facts is often determined by the notions of discourse analysis. The term *discourse* can be understood in different ways by different scholars, but in general, *discourse* is understood as a group of texts. For example, a set of texts of one topic can be defined as a discourse.

Discourse has a spatial and temporal extent. The parameter of space has to do with a single, unified territory united by such factors as language and culture in the broadest sense. The time parameter means that a chronology must be defined, within which the set of texts that we perceive as discourse is formed.

The unity of space and time in determining the boundaries of discourse suggests the possibility of designating a set of cultural phenomena by discourse. For example, the totality of texts about the creation and driving of passenger cars today (including TV programs) creates modern car discourse. If we compare modern auto discourse, including advertisements, songs (at least Serega's "Black Boomer") and numerous auto shows, with the auto discourse of the beginning of the last century, it becomes clear that the range of analysis of this discourse is extremely wide.

M. Foucault's famous definition of discourse as a set of texts belonging to the same formation is fruitful. In this case, the *formation is* understood as a spatial and temporal identification permeated by a single ideology.

This understanding of the two key terms of modern linguistics, *linguistic personality* and *discourse*, suggests that the language of a certain personality type forms a clearly delineated discourse.

L. Wisson points out: "The peculiarities of the English language of America and its culture, which are extremely important for students of this language, are the result of more than 300 years of history, opened in 1620 by the arrival of the Pilgrims on the ship *Mayflower*" (4, p. 29). It would seem that we are talking about quite understandable things, nevertheless, this text requires a special analysis from the point of view of our ideas about discourse. Firstly, it is unambiguously stated that knowledge (even if brilliant) of English does not guarantee mutual understanding of the addressee in America. Therefore, L. Wisson does not limit himself to pointing out the importance of knowing the peculiarities, but introduces the expressive indexer *exclusively*, exceptionally important.

The extreme importance of knowing America's idiosyncrasies, language and culture, actually means that without knowledge of these idiosyncrasies, you will be misunderstood. Despite your perfect command of the English language.

Secondly, it follows that a country's language and its culture form a single and integral discourse. It is impossible to understand a country's language outside its culture. In this case, both factors mentioned above are actualized again, i.e. both space and time are actualized. In this case, the space of the USA at a certain historical stage. The unity of space and time automatically implies the ideology of this unified space-time. This understanding of discourse makes the notion of formation natural, i.e. a discourse is a group of texts belonging to a single formation.

It follows from all of the above that the linguocultural aspect of the study of discourse is the most important. Moreover, the definition of discourse at the intersection of such concepts as time, space and culture orientates the researcher to the study of culture as the most important means of understanding language.

Apparently, the totality of these factors was in M. Pesce's mind when he wrote that "there are methods of analysis that *seemingly have nothing to* do with linguistics, they appeared first and developed around the time of the above-described upheaval, which, due to the lack of time distance, they did not notice. These methods are used in an attempt to answer the question of the meaning of the text in its, if I may say so, "pre-Sussurian" form: they stand outside modern linguistics, which does not mean that they do not rely on concepts of linguistic origin - just that these concepts are outside modern linguistic theory" (14, p. 304).

If we are really talking about *modern linguistics*, then all these pre-Sussurian methods become relevant again. If we mean cognitive linguistics, then analyzing linguistic facts according to the model of perception, information processing and representation has always been relevant in linguistics.

Apparently, discourse analysis is labeled as *pre-Sussurian for the* reason that it is not interested in immediate constituents as purely linguistic entities, i.e. signs. However, the *sign* itself is then defined as something completely artificial. In other words, we perceive a sign as something possessing significance solely by virtue of its relations with other signs within the linguistic system. Outside the system of signs, a sign is meaningless at all.

Cognitive analysis assumes that the sign is meaningful outside the sign system. Moreover, it is meaningful outside the sign system in the first place. It follows that a sign is not something definite only by virtue of its relations with other signs, but something self-contained by virtue of the manifestation of ethnic experience.

The cognitive model as an epistemological tool says quite unambiguously that every linguistic sign should be analyzed as a product of the collective thinking and experience of the ethnos that uses this sign. Consequently, each sign is interesting in itself as such a product and has absolute value.

With this approach, form and content in language become more independent, their independent value increases.

The linguistic personality, analyzed from the point of view of discursive values, acts as a carrier of culture, cultural values. It is important to keep in mind that it is legitimate and reasonable to understand culture as any space of meaning, goals and attitudes, standards and etiquettes, rituals and stamps.

The study of linguistic personality as a combination of these factors makes both linguistic personality itself and its study a socially significant phenomenon. If we talk about the linguistic personality represented in fiction texts, the linguocultural aspect is prominently represented here. Moreover, linguistic personality is framed as such solely due to the reality of linguocultural features. This means that the peculiarities of a character's speech, even within the framework of the typology of characters, are determined precisely by the attitude to culture as a system of special values. The peculiarity of speech as such is determined against the background of the culture's value system. This is somewhat reminiscent of Sossurian significance, defined solely as a bundle of differential features. As for linguocultural significance, it too presupposes the existence of culture as a value system. However, this in no way detracts from the absolute value of a cultural reality or artifact as a result of mastering the surrounding world by an ethnos.

Thus, the linguistic personality studied in the aspect of discourse analysis is perceived as a persona-type possessing a characteristic discourse. Directly, the components of such discourse are perceived not as signs-elements of the language-system of signs, but as linguocultural values that have absolute value from the point of view of the experience of the individual and ethnos and relative value from the point of view of the cultural system.

The cultural system is largely standard, hence the linguistic person in discourse reproduces what has been initiated by the cultural field. On the other hand, the linguistic personality in discourse creates something that was not known before it and thus becomes exactly its characteristic property. Consequently, the study of linguistic personality in the aspect of discourse analysis is oriented both to the study of culture, to the study of standards and types of speech behavior, and to the definition of the framework of what is nowadays commonly defined as linguistic personality.

7. SPEECH CHARACTERIZATION AND LINGUISTIC PERSONALITY

In this paper we aim to analyze the speech of the characters in F. S. Fitzgerald's story "A Diamond the Size of the Ritz Hotel" from the point of view of manifestation of linguistic personality traits. We analyze a fragment of the story in which one of the main characters named Percy explains to his friend John how rich his father is. Here we should pay special attention to John's reaction, which is extremely significant from the point of view of linguistic personality. To Percy's entire tirade, he makes a naive exclamation. John is completely naive, but in that naivete he is also all American. He admits completely unashamedly that he is very fond of rich people. This phrase manifests the very essence of the American mentality. And it is important to understand that this mentality is realized outside of morality. There can be no assessments like "good" or "bad" here. It is neither bad nor good. This is the way it is, and Americans are like this.

"He must be very rich" (25, p. 7), says John, and in these words there is one naked delight. "I'm glad." It is not at all clear what he is glad about. Indeed, you can't be glad about someone else's wealth. "I like very rich people" (25, p. 7), he adds.

All three sentences characterize John, on the one hand, as an extremely simple-minded guy, on the other hand, as a true representative of the civilization in question. Perhaps this is an artistic device, and John's naivete is programmatic in nature. Perhaps F. S. Fitzgerald is laughing by putting into John's mouth the phrase that he loves very rich people. Nevertheless, these phrases reflect the standards of the country. In the last century, it was in America that such a theory as behaviorism was created. Here is not the place to delve into this psychological theory. Let us only note that within the framework of this theory, human behavior is interpreted as a reaction to certain stimuli. We can know about these stimuli, and then human behavior is explainable, we can not know and in this case we do not understand the motives of actions. However, stimuli, explicit or implicit, always exist.

Behaviorism has also influenced linguistics. More precisely, linguistics has used the methodology of behaviorism for its purposes, which was quite fruitful. It should also be noted that in the conditions of formation of methods and principles of cognitive linguistics, the achievements of behaviorism are successfully combined with cognitivism. In other words, if stimuli and reactions are repeated in the space of this or that culture, they can quite naturally be regarded as standards of this culture. Standard reactions to identical stimuli should be regarded as manifestations of national mentality.

If Percy's confession is confusing, John's declaration of love is equally unexpected. However, both are unexpected only in the space of the work of fiction. This unexpectedness is an authorial device. The tasks of linguistic or linguocultural description do not include the interpretation of literary devices. In the space of linguocultural description, the speech of literary characters is evaluated from the point of view of the national-linguistic picture of the world. And everything is quite understandable here. John's naivety has a narrative character, i.e. he, directly expressing his sympathies, appears as the most typical representative of the corresponding culture and the most typical bearer of the corresponding mentality.

We should also pay special attention to this *very thing*. That is, he loves not just rich people, but people who are very rich. It is also important that we are talking about a feeling of love. John does not say that he respects very rich people for their success. He doesn't say he bows down to them. He loves them, and love is a selfless feeling. If we try to extrapolate this situation to the national mentality, we have to admit that John has nothing to do with it, it is America that adores very rich people. Thus, John turns out to be just a sign that testifies to the character of the culture he represents.

One can speculate a great deal about the motivations behind this love. The background information here is extremely broad. It would be appropriate to recall the world experience and not to connect the worship of wealth exclusively with the national psychology of the people in question. A classic example, designed for all times, is the biblical story of the golden calf, which people immediately begin to worship as soon as the prophet leaves them. The background information on this topic is virtually inexhaustible. However, for the purposes of linguistic analysis, the amount of it that contributes to the understanding of the text is sufficient. As for linguocultural analysis, it is certainly only with the culture of linguistic personalities that it can connect the text. In other words, it is not just information about man's worship of gold that is directly behind the text, but spatial and temporal cultural and cultural information. Space is America, time is the beginning of the last century. Consequently, it is this amount of background information that is in demand, as it outlines the contours of the linguistic personality.

At a deep semantic level, worship and love are different concepts. It is worth turning to popular lexicographical sources in order to accurately visualize what kind of feeling we are dealing with when it comes to love. In S. I. Ozhegov's Dictionary of the Russian Language, the meaning of the word *love is* defined as follows: "LOVE 1. A feeling of selfless and deep affection, heartfelt attraction. 2. Tendency, predilection for something". (13, с. 335).

Indeed, the deep affection that Americans feel for very rich people is completely unselfish. After all, these people do not bestow anything on their adorers. Envy is probably more standard in this situation. However, it is the deep and bright feeling of love that is characteristic of genuine

Americans. Of course, the semesemes presented in S. I. Ozhegov's Dictionary are related at a very deep level. On a superficial level, "fondness" is not so obviously motivated by "the feeling of selfless affection", but the sememe "passion" organically accommodates them in one epistemological model. Thus, one phrase reveals the essence of linguistic personality at a very deep level. It is worth emphasizing once again that the linguistic personality is adequate to the cultural personality, if not identical to it.

In this fragment, F. S. Fitzgerald pushes the expression, but he is quite right. By increasing the expressive level of the text, he manages to show how sincere John is. It would seem that what else can be added to such a discursive confession as what this guy has allowed himself. Nevertheless, after the phrase *I like very rich people* he adds *the richer a fella is, the better I like him.* That is, there is no limit to John's love. He states that how much richer a person is, the more he loves him. No matter how much he loves a very rich man, if he meets a richer man, he will love him more. All of these phrases complete the person's appearance and create a picture of not only the person, but also a picture of the world.

F.S. Fitzgerald writes that John's face flushes with passion, he is oblivious, he speaks as if in a trance and is completely truthful. He uses sustained comparisons peculiar to the relevant discourse on gemstones. Thus, he speaks of rubies as big as hen's eggs: "Schnlitzer-Murphy had rubies as big as hen's eggs" (25, p. 7). The comparison of sapphires with balls looks original against this background: "and sapphires that were like globes with lights on them". It is clear that originality is inherent in John's speech, not the writer's. This comparison is put into his mouth in order to demonstrate the extent of his delight.

As we can see, the hyperbolic style is supported by John. However, Percy, after impressing his friend, begins to play the solidity game. It is, of course, motivated by his confidence in his own position and its firmness. He says that he likes jewelry too, has managed to amass a good collection, but would not want the school to know about it.

Percy's speech is peppered with both enthusiastic responses to John's remarks and his own pseudo-restrained remarks. In this context, it is particularly significant that Percy tells John about his father's wealth without much emotion. Equally easily he speaks of the diamond, which is utterly fantastic. When John continues to rave about how he has seen diamonds the size of walnuts at Schnlitzer-Murphy's, Percy calmly drops, "That's nothing," i.e., it's nothing. His father has a diamond bigger than the Ritz-Carlton Hotel: "My father has a diamond bigger than the Ritz-Carlton Hotel" (25, p. 7).

Percy's calmness and self-confidence, solidity are again replaced by expressive hyperbolization. If John compares rubies to chicken eggs, sapphires to balls, and diamonds to walnuts, Percy compares his father's diamond to the standard of magnitude - the Ritz-Carlton Hotel. However, he himself realizes that this is quite unusual. Therefore, he lowers his voice to a whisper when he informs John about the diamond.

The theme of enormity and brilliance continues. After such a significant dialogue between John and Percy, in which each of them is unambiguously revealed as a linguistic and cultural-social personality, hyperbolization is clearly presented in the author's speech. It is also significant that the splendor of wealth is realized against the background of poverty of the inhabitants of Fish, where the friends arrive. The final moment of these fragments of the text is the impression that the car that has come to pick them up makes on John. The sheer enormity of the automobile plays an iconic role. Of course, the author's words conveying John's impression are actually John's. F. S. Fitzgerald conveys his inner speech. The body of the automobile was of some shiny metal. John says it was darker in color than nickel and lighter than silver. I wonder if it was platinum! As for the glass, John was frightened at even the thought of what it was, as it looked like diamonds. Thus, John finds himself entirely at the mercy of a magical fairy tale, a fairy tale entirely created by the American dream of untold wealth.

Characteristic of a representative of an extremely wealthy house is also Percy's next remark that no one should see such a car. The young man's snobbery is also evident in this fragment of his speech, but this time it is characterized by the healthy sobriety of a man who is aware of his social and property status and understands the undesirable impression his wealth may make on others. He asks John to forgive him for having to shake in the baby carriage because a carriage came to the station to pick them up: "but of course it wouldn't do for the people on the train or those Godforsaken fellas in Fish to see this automobile" (25, p. 9). Here he reveals both the sobriety of a man who understands the need to protect his wealth from prying eyes, but also the snobbery generated by the consciousness of his own inaccessibility. Here he is characterized by the expression *Godforsaken*, literally meaning "forgotten by God, abandoned by God to his fate".

However, these polar connotations are not the only ones that make up the essence of the fragment. It is significant that the completely neutral expression *people is* also localized between them. In other words, Percy, in a style completely devoid of emotionality, says, as a matter of course, that it is inadmissible that people on the train should see this car. This phrase is highly characteristic of the linguistic personality of such people. In this case, it is not trivial envy or ill-will that they fear. They understand well that "others" should not even suppose about the existence of such things in the world. The desire to boast about something ends here. Such a fantastic car can stun others, and the stun in turn can move them to unforeseen actions.

Once in the car, John continues to let out exclamations of delight: "Gosh! What a car!"

F.S.Fitzgerald describes the interior of the fantastic car, which is really able to cause delight. The seats are covered with unique tapestries, the covers are studded with diamonds. The situation is quite extraordinary, but Percy remains true to himself. He laughs and says it's old junk: "Percy laughed. "Why, it's just an old junk we use for a station wagon" (25, p. 9). That is, Percy's family uses this luxury car solely as transportation for the station wagon. The automobile is sent to the station to deliver people and goods.

Percy's speech is interspersed with solid remarks that orient John, opening his eyes to the world, and the dismissive remarks of a snob who allows himself to ridicule everything that stuns others. After he calls the luxurious, jeweled and tapestried automobile a *shambles,* he gives him completely neutral and emotionally unexpressed information. He prepares his friend for what he is about to see and warns him: "it's not going to be like anything you've ever seen before.

In this place of the text, F.S. Fitzgerald somewhat departs from the narrative principles of the image and begins to explain John's behavior. In our opinion, this slightly weakens the artistic power of the image and, accordingly, the idea of the linguistic and cultural personality manifested in the image of this young man. All of John's lines so far have presupposed an interpretation against a cultural and social background. The fragment saturated with youthful delight, the writer concludes with a discursive interpretation: "The simple piety prevalent in Hades has the earnest worship of and respect for riches as the first article of its creed" (25, p. 9).

The connotation of the text and the sincerely expressed irony do not weaken the very meaning of the statement. In other words, the expression here does not outweigh the meaning. F. S. Fitzgerald quite clearly says that the town in which John grew up prays to only one god - wealth. It is as if the writer does not trust his addressee and begins to explain the reason for his hero's rapture. Although John's phrase that he loves rich people very much was quite sufficient for a proper interpretation of the discourse. Moreover, he is very fond of very rich people. F.S. Fitzgerald emphasizes John's sincerity, i.e. all the inhabitants of Gades sincerely worship wealth. This is their naive, perhaps even primitive piety. It is their main commandment, the most important point, the dogma of their faith. In drawing a parallel between the naive feelings of the inhabitants of the province and comparing their immediate emotions with the dogmas of their faith, the writer is, of course, ironic. At the same time, however, he is absolutely serious. In fact, he here shifts from the position of an artist to that of a moralizer. What is important for us is that the discursive interpretation of the author is fully superimposed on the characteristics of the linguistic personality.

8. THE LINGUISTIC PERSONALITY OF CHARACTERS IN A WORK OF FICTION AS A DOCUMENT OF EPOCH AND LANGUAGE

As an object of analysis we chose the story "The diamond as big as the Ritz" by the American writer F. S. Fitzgerald. A special place in the structure of F. S. Fitzgerald's narrative is occupied by the image of the boy Percy. The skill of the writer is manifested, in particular, in the fact that Percy's speech is naturally superimposed on the description of his appearance, which is written out most carefully. Both have linguocultural significance. Moreover, as far as appearance is concerned, not only facial features and figure, but also inner qualities are presented. Thus, it is noted that he was *handsome* and quiet - *handsome* and *quiet*. Besides, he was *pleasant in manner*. All these qualities are very important not only for Americans, but also for the Western man in general. Just the Americans, according to the popular perception of them, are rather rude and rather noisy. Therefore, the indication that Percy was quiet and not only well-mannered but also pleasant to be around is symbolically significant. If we translate these characteristics to an explicit level, it turns out that Percy was un-American in his socializing. If Americans are noisy, Percy is the quiet one. If they are rude, this boy is exquisitely polite.

As you can see, characterization breaks down into the external and internal. It is extremely important how Percy is dressed. He is *exceedingly well dressed*. This means that he is not just well or excellently dressed, but dressed with the utmost care. The author specifically emphasizes that this was extraordinary even for St. Midas School.

It is also significant that Percy keeps aloof from the other boys. Why he does this seems to remain a mystery. The author notes that he shuns his comrades for reasons that are unclear. Clearly, this is just intrigue, and in fact, everything is clear. Percy is not just rich, he is fantastically rich.

Percy's speech complements his external and internal characteristics. The first phrase he utters in the story denotes the extent of his father's wealth. And characteristically, he abruptly interrupts neutral conversations about his school friends. At first on the train, Percy and John talk about school and school friends. It is noted that he talks on the train, becoming unlike the ordinary Percy that John had known up to this point. Suddenly, Percy utters a key phrase: "My father," he said, "is by far the richest man in the world" (25, p. 7). It is not only the decisiveness of the turn in the conversation that draws attention, but also the unappealing tone.

In this phrase, significant background information is simultaneously actualized. It is the spatial, temporal, cultural and cultural information that allows us to understand and appreciate both the suddenness of the change in the topic of conversation and its emphasis, and the stylistics of Percy's statement.

Certainly, Percy's speech is quite deliberately oriented towards the evaluation by his own addressee. In the eyes of Americans, wealth has a special enchanting power. Of course, it can be said that this is the unconscious attitude to wealth of all people. This is indeed true, but American standards must be taken into account. It is perhaps the only nation in the world for whom external success has such an enchanting power. As for the symbol of success, it is certainly wealth. Great and steady wealth is not perceived elementally as a lot of money, but as the power and significance of a person who has managed to achieve everything in life. Therefore, when Percy says that there is no one in the world richer than his father, he means to say that there is no one in the world better than his father, there is no one stronger and smarter than him and there cannot be.

The expression *by far has* a serious expressive function here. It seems that Percy was holding back from the last possible effort all this time at school. He kept thinking about how he would tell John that his father was the richest man in the world. Context also implies a psychological interpretation of the speaker's personality. Such a factor as intimization should be taken into account. Percy says that his father is certainly the richest man in the world, but he wants to say that he is the best man in the world, extending this superiority to himself and to all those who are related to them - ancestors, family members, etc.

Of course, the analysis may go beyond the textual space proper and in this sense be unjustified, but it is quite logical to extrapolate the findings on intimization to the American mentality. A characteristic feature of the American mentality is a sense of inclusion in the achievements of one's own civilization. In this sense, an in-depth analysis of Percy's phrase reveals its psychological background, which in turn manifests the essence of the American character. Thus, what is conceptually significant for the linguistic personality here is the feeling of superiority and, moreover, the absence of doubt in one's own superiority.

The concept of "superiority" is not revealed as a result of hermeneutic analysis, but is discursively expressed in the text of the story. Thus, John's response to this categorical statement was as delicate as he himself. John says merely "Oh." However, however expressionless this "Oh" may be on the lexico-semantic level, it is quite meaningful in the consituation. It is associated with surprise, and with surprise both at the statement itself and at its frankness. It is also intended to express delight, which should be regarded as approval. On the other hand, the "O" is a reaction to the categorical nature of Percy's statement, in which sense it can also be interpreted as doubt.

In connection with this phrase, which characterizes Percy's linguistic consciousness, another thought can be made. The phrase that his father is the richest man in the world, and there is no doubt about it, in our opinion, constitutes the climax of the story. It absorbs all the linguistic and extra-linguistic nuances of the actual information. Everything that came before it is completely insignificant from the point of view of textual expression. Everything that follows this phrase is an elementary unfolding of the fabula. When we speak of the climactic content of the phrase, we mean not a literary and artistic moment, but a linguistic or linguocultural one.

To conclude this fragment, it should be noted that Percy does not limit himself to this phrase, despite all its significance and categorical nature. He repeats it: 'By far the richest,' repeated Persy" (25, p. 7).

Of course, a psychoanalyst would say that he was trying to convince himself, not John. Nevertheless, the repetition of the phrase is as significant as the phrase itself.

The phrases that follow are extremely characteristic of Percy's linguistic personality. Incidentally, it must be said that everything John says is equally characteristic of him. Therefore, the conversation between the friends is quite important in terms of the linguistic characterization of both of them. Thus, John says that he read in the World Almanac that the annual income of one person living in America is five million dollars a year. There are four other people earning four million each.

It is significant that John draws his information from the World Almanac. This, firstly, characterizes him as a "reading boy". Secondly, as a boy who is disconnected from life. Another detail is important in the text. The World Almanac, published in America, focuses on the states of individuals. This information is published, people, even children, are interested in it. The extralinguistic detail is that earning five million a year was a huge achievement even for America between the two world wars. Only one person could have achieved such success. On the other hand, it also says a lot about the money itself. After all, the point of the information is not just that one lucky person made five million a year. The point is that at that time five million was a fabulous sum.

There is certainly an element of hyperbolization in the story. Hyperbolization is discursively stated already in the title, which suggests that there may be a diamond the size of the Ritz Hotel. In the course of the story we realize that this diamond is actually a mountain. Thus, F.S. Fitzgerald essentially creates a mythological or folkloric image. The central image and consequently the linguistic personality of the story is Percy, as it is he who maintains this perspective of hyperbole. The hyperbolic style and content is emphasized all the time, both in his appearance and in the speech of this young man.

In this context, both Percy's linguistic and paralinguistic reaction to John's excursion into the World Almanac is perfectly understandable. Percy calls the richest people in the country, and therefore, as implied, the world, *petty* names. The expressions used are characteristic. He says *they're nothing*

(25, p. 7). That is, they are just empty space, they are nothing.

He uses an even stronger expression: *catch-penny capitalists* (25, p. 7). Here it is absolutely necessary to reveal the internal form of the sign, as it is actualized. *Catch* means "to catch", penny is an exoticism well known to the Russian-speaking reader as well. A penny is a small coin. Consequently, Percy calls the richest people of his country penny catchers, i.e. beggars, beggars. Here again we see the mechanism of hyperbolization at work. Since it is directly connected with the image of Percy, it becomes a distinctive feature of his speech. His whole being expresses contempt for the *best people of the country*, therefore, "speaking down" is not situational. It is a quality of permanent significance.

It can be assumed that the "manking" of society and its values is important not only for Percy, but also for F. S. Fitzgerald himself. This interesting feature is equally stylistically relevant for both Percy and the author. The only difference is that Percy's linguistic personality is organically woven from such phrases. As for F. S. Fitzgerald himself, it is more of a language game for him. However, it should be taken into account that even in the case of a language game, the author creates real constructions directly associated with the national mentality and linguistic picture of the world. For example, the fact that Percy's father is fabulously rich and the richest man in America is much poorer than him is not in itself a sufficient reason for such global contempt. The point is that this contempt constitutes the content not only of this boy, but of the country as a whole. And if this is indeed the case, then both action and speech act as merely a standard model in the text, or rather, one of the standard models directly related to world-understanding. Percy does not even simply understand the world in this way; he perceives it in this way on an unconscious level.

F.S. Fitzgerald intensifies the expression, it is not enough for him to put into Percy's mouth the expression "catchers or grabbers of pennies", i.e. small coins. He uses another equally strong expression. Percy says that these so-called representatives of the financial elite are in fact *financial small-fry*. The lexico-semantic whole created is characterized by both semantic and stylistic, expressive, saturation. Besides, the expression has a vivid internal form, it creates a whole picture. Calling millionaires *trifles, small fish,* Percy implicitly introduces such a standard as "shark". That is, his father is a shark, which is understandable even without the definition of *financial.*

In the fragment from F.S. Fitzgerald's story under consideration, despite its insignificance, the linguistic personality accumulates a huge historical and cultural volume of information, actually broadly manifests the linguistic picture characterizing the mentality of the people, civilization and a particular social stratum.

9. LINGUISTIC PERSONALITY OF THE AUTHOR OF A FICTION TEXT

Artistic work gives an opportunity to differentiate the linguistic personality of the author-creator of the text and the personality of the image represented in the language. The former is most often unconscious and involves hermeneutic analysis. The linguistic personality of the character is consciously constructed. In other words, the author of the text cannot go beyond himself as a speaking personality. Whatever and however he writes about, the author reveals himself as a linguistic personality, established in a certain space and time. The text may contain the image of a narrator, also constructed by the writer and which it is inappropriate to confuse with the real creator of the text. In this article, we are interested in the writer's linguistic personality directly.

We will analyze the linguistic personality of the author of the fiction text on the material of Francis Scott Fitzgerald's story "The Diamond as Big as the Ritz".

As cultural prerequisites for the analysis, it can be noted that F.S. Fitzgerald came from a well-to-do American family. In addition, his great-great-grandfather was the author of the U.S. anthem. Thus, the writer belonged to the people who created the country and the mentality of its inhabitants. He studied in elite educational institutions, which also left an imprint on his character. Let us turn to the analysis. The linguistic appearance of the narrator is revealed from the first lines of the story.

"John T. Unger came from a family that had been well known in Hades - a small town on the Mississippi River - for several generations. John's father had held the amateur golf championship through many a heated contest; Mrs. Unger was known "from hot-box to hot-bed," as the local phrase went, for her political addresses; and young John T. Unger, who had just turned sixteen, had danced all the latest dances from New York before he put on long trousers. And now, for a certain time, he was to be away from home. That respect for a New England education which is the bane of all provincial places, which drains them yearly of their most promising young men, had seized upon his parents. Nothing would suit them but that he should go to St. Midas's School near Boston - Hades was too small to hold their darling and gifted son" (25, p. 5).

Already this small introduction to the story is extremely characteristic of the addressee of American history. The key signs of discourse are such words as *Hades, several generations, golf championship, heated contest, from hot-box to hot-bed, political addresses, had danced all the latest dances from New York, away from home, respect for a New England education, bane of all provincial places, drains, seized upon his parents, nothing would suit them, Hades was too small to hold their darling and gifted son.*

As we can see, quite a few words and expressions fulfill the role of key words and expressions in this text. Some of them have a deep conceptual character. There are even hyperlinks in the text, designed for a well-educated reader. For example, this is the hyperlink that ends this short introductory fragment. The expression *Hades was too small to hold their darling and gifted son* unambiguously correlates with Philip of Macedon's enthusiastic remark to his son Alexander, who had just tamed the mad Bucephalus: "Find a kingdom worthy of you, my son. Macedonia is too small for you!"

The fragment implicitly contains the characteristics of elitist American society. This is the narrator's position as a linguistic person; he does it easily and simply. But it also contains an explicit ironic attitude towards this elitist position. This is already a conscious attitude of the author as a linguistic personality. The last sentence unambiguously characterizes this point. The replica has a veiled character, but it is quite obvious. At the same time, it characterizes a person who has received a good education and studied the history of Ancient Greece.

The sentence is an intertext, even if indirectly related to the situation in Ancient Macedonia. The sentence highlights key words and concepts. These are words such as *too, small, to hold,* here *to* accommodate, *gifted,* and *son.*

It is very important for the hyperlink that the city is not just small, but too small, since "too" directly correlates with "son". It is for him that it is not just small, but too small: "Macedonia is too small for you". In this context *too* fulfills an obvious expressive load, as it is informationally quite *small.*

If Alexander conquered Bucephalus, then the associative sign here is *gifted.*

The name of the city of *Hades is* symbolic from the point of view of the linguistic person as a carrier of a certain culture. It is not by chance that it is said that Western culture is based on two whales: ancient culture and Christianity. Hades means Hades, the underworld or the realm of the dead. The association with the ancient Greek Hades is quite obvious. At the explicit level only the name is presented, but as a culturally meaningful sign, *Hades* makes a very large amount of background information demanded. It is clear that much depends on the addressee's awareness, but regardless of the addressee and the degree of his awareness, the sign *Hades* represents the entire volume of cultural and culturological information.

Despite the fact that *Hades* has the same denotation, at the significative level it is possible to distinguish two directions, each of which forms its own associative space. Thus, the first associative direction forms the signifier "the kingdom of the dead", the second - "the underground kingdom". In both cases, the same associative mechanism worked for the ancient Greeks. In the space of an artistic text both directions are relevant, as they unfold a different semantic field.

Hades is associated with the realm of the dead because the author considers the upper class of this city, not just people, to be dead. Here, incidentally, biblical associations are also actualized. For example, when Christ calls his disciple to come with him, and he says that he will bury his father and follow him, Christ says to him, "Follow me and let the dead bury their own dead" (Gospel of Matthew 8:22).

This section of the Gospel is never clearly understood. Christ calls anyone who is far from the search for truth a *dead man*. Let us also recall Marcel Proust's widely known expression that "life is an effort in time." In other words, when one simply enjoys life, one is not living. Thus, Western European culture and mentality has developed a view of life as an effort to achieve significant results. Simply living, without strenuous physical and spiritual labor, is existence, being. In this case, the semantic field unfolded by the concept "kingdom of the dead" is specifically actualized by the author.

It is also important that we are not talking about the dead, but about their kingdom. The kingdom is associated with the state, i.e. here is not just a cemetery where dead people lie, but a state in which they conduct some business, rule, quarrel, consider themselves superior or inferior to someone and even dream about something. There is no effort in time. Consequently, there is no life. Maybe it is the vague feeling of no life that makes parents think that this city is too small for their son and cannot accommodate him with all his talents.

The concept "underground kingdom", as noted, in the actual context is not identical to the "kingdom of the dead". The concept is primarily intended to characterize an unbearable territory. It is not by chance that the text goes on to say that John was teased at school and was always asked how they were doing down there, whether it was too hot.

Both concepts and their actualization in the context unambiguously characterize the author's mentality, or rather, represent him as a person formed under the direct influence of European spirituality. It is also important to note the interweaving of mythological, historical-cultural and Christian motifs. Another characteristic detail is that this information is hidden and is revealed only as a result of hermeneutic analysis.

The seemingly completely neutral expression also unambiguously characterizes the author, but already as a typical American and, moreover, as a representative or scion of an elite American family.

The understanding that culture is the work of many generations has always characterized the Western European mentality and distinguished it from the worldview of many other nations. For example, the great A. S. Pushkin always compared Russia with Western Europe in this respect and came to disappointing conclusions: "Disrespect for names sanctified by glory (the first sign of ignorance and weak-mindedness), unfortunately, is considered not only allowed, but also commendable prowess" (15, p. 278).

As the most important economic foundation of English conservatism, it is necessary to recall the entail. It was the majorat that formed historically the economic basis of the cultural tradition that led Western Europe to prosperity. In saying that John came from a family that had been renowned and respected in Gades for generations, F.S. Fitzgerald introduces an extremely serious motif. In the context of the discourse that the author creates, it means that John's family was one of the families that created this Hades. Consequently, they were carriers of the culture that characterized this place.

The expression *golf championship* unambiguously characterizes the author as a linguistic personality. It is even difficult to determine from the context whether the indication of this circumstance has an unconscious-narrative character or it is a conscious sketch, a character trait characterizing him as a representative of a certain culture and class of this culture. Golf is a game of rich Americans, so the word *golf* in the consciousness of the informed addressee is unambiguously associated with America and Americans. Another significant detail is the indication that John's father held the golf championship for several years in a row. This is far from neutral information. The implicitly presented signal suggests that John's father devoted a lot of time and energy to golf if he could hold that championship.

By itself, the expression *heated contest* in a neutral context would say nothing. However, it is necessary to analyze this expression in the context of the unfolding discourse. The key word here is, of course, *heated, as* it is associated with Gades and is included in the paradigm of signs denoting "heat", "fire", "unbearable", etc.

The same paradigm includes the expression *from hot-box to hot-bed.* Here it means that John's mother made political speeches, which were characterized by turbulence and emotionality. The expression *hot-box* means a steam boiler, *hot-bed means a* greenhouse. As we can see, the theme of "heat" continues and intensifies.

The seemingly neutral expression *political addresses* also reveals a close connection with the cultural and historical context and unambiguously characterizes the narrator's linguistic personality. The mentioned word combination can be considered quite usual from the point of view of not only American, but also Western European culture in general. This culture is directly related to the phenomenon that in the West is called the history of democracy. Political speeches, so common in ancient Greece, become the standard of public life in the United States. The text is particularly expressive because of the female character involved in the public debate. The background information behind this sign differs both in volume and quality, as the history of the women's movement, in particular the suffragettes, is at the same time in demand. Thus Mrs. Unger was known from the steamers to the steamers for her political speeches. In one stroke, F. S. Fitzgerald creates a typical image of a middle-class American provincial, or even a local aristocrat.

In American culture throughout the twentieth century, dancing has held a special place. This art form was particularly popular, and at the same time the ability to dance fashionable dances was considered a calling card of a quite modern person. F.S. Fitzgerald about young John says that he *had danced all the latest dances from New York.* It is very important here that he danced all the latest, i.e. new dances, and that these dances were from New York. The implicit information is that if John had been in New York, he would have rubbed the nose of the capital's dandies. Another indication that Gades is too small for him.

A completely meaningless phrase about the need to leave home acquires a symbolic meaning in the context of American culture. Phrases like *away from home* are not just standards of American literature and cinema, they reflect the linguistic picture of the world. The constituent *away* plays a special role here. Perhaps it would be more correct to perceive this phrase in accordance with the internal form of this word: *away from home.* There is also a huge amount of cultural information behind this expression. The American pioneers were called *pioneers* because they traveled around the country on wagons. The image of the courageous pioneer, familiar to us from the novels of F. Cooper, J. London, and other writers, thrills American youth to this day. Thus, John's departure from home acquires a new meaning in the context of the American history of exploration of the wild West.

Against the background of the expressions discussed above, *respect for a New England education* looks quite harmless. The phrase really has a universal character. The point is that at all times rich provincials considered the province to be a closed space for themselves, which meant an unambiguously failed destiny. All provincials at all times sought to go "beyond" the province. If they did not succeed themselves, they should try for the sake of their children. Consequently, piety before the central education is a common thing. However, even in this case there is a significant background behind the phrase in question.

It is characteristic of Americans to adore their own civilization. And since in the Western mind civilization has always been associated with education, it is clear that *respect for a New England education is* a perfectly natural phenomenon. Of course, the background information includes the idea of serious investment in education, so characteristic of America. The standard situation is that activities in which a lot of money is invested are extremely attractive. No matter how crude and practical Americans might look in the eyes of Europeans, it was Americans who had the idea of investing huge amounts of capital in an endeavor that only turns a profit decades later.

When F.S. Fitzgerald speaks about *respect for a New England education*, he does not mean only the common human society's desire to give children a good education. *New England education* is key to the demand for background information. The analysis shows that it is precisely the attitude of American culture to education and science that is in question.

At the same time, American thinking makes the writer soberly assess the situation. He realizes that the thirst to go beyond one'*s* own cultural surroundings and native habitat naturally leads to the *bane of all provincial places*. The desire for education as it is characteristic of America forces the best to leave the province and literally run away from home.

The situation is familiar to us even from the novels of O. de Balzac. Rastignac and Lucien de Ruebampre. Thousands of young men leave their homes in the hope of conquering Paris. Today, this theme is exploited by Russian cinematography. Despite the universality of the theme, its universal character, in our opinion, in F.S.Fitzgerald's story it actualizes purely American spatial and temporal information. All-American patriotism makes F.S. Fitzgerald simultaneously regret that the piety for education in New England is literally drying up the province.

The writer, like any patriot, is an idealist; he wants all American lands to develop in parallel.

Of course, it is not by chance that such an expressive word as *drain is* used in this context. The level of textual expression directly characterizes the writer's attitude to the described fact. The desire to get a New England education is drying up the province.

The author's linguistic personality is consistently revealed throughout the artistic discourse. In fact, the whole text implies a consistent hermeneutic analysis. However, the material considered gives a clear idea of the writer's personality, which is the result of quite certain socio-historical and cultural conditions. It is quite obvious that this personality is represented in language, which alone can be a reliable indicator of social and cultural characteristics.

10. AMERICAN HAPPINESS, AMERICAN LIFESTYLE AND LINGUISTIC IDENTITY IN U.S. FICTION

Today it is no longer a secret that Americans have created not just a "New World", a new nation, but also a new worldview. Americans do not just speak a new variant of English, but also claim a new mentality represented in American English. Consequently, in terms of the new linguistic paradigm, we can say that the American nation is the bearer of its own and unique linguistic picture of the world. The peculiarities of this linguistic picture of the world are clearly manifested in the linguistic personality of Americans. As for the linguistic personality, it is difficult to find a more vivid representation of it than fiction. It is in fiction that linguistic personality is represented in all its socio-historical and socio-cultural aspects. In our opinion, the linguistic personality of this country is very convexly represented in the works of F. C. Fitzgerald. These two writers were able to organically reflect the inner world of their characters, the personality of the native and typical representative of their country, social, cultural and linguistic personality.

For example, in the story "A Diamond the Size of the Ritz Hotel", F. S. Fitzgerald writes the following: "Now in Hades - as you know if you ever have been there - the names of the more fashionable preparatory schools and colleges mean very little. The inhabitants have been so long out of the world that, though they make a show of keeping up-to-date in dress and manners and literature, they depend to a great extent on hearsay, and a function that in Hades would be considered elaborate would doubtless be hailed by a Chicago beef-princess as 'perhaps a little tacky.'" (25, c. 5).

In this fragment F. S. Fitzgerald recommends himself as a representative of the American elite. The elitism of the linguistic personality is unambiguously manifested both in the content of the text and in its stylistics. Particularly characteristic in this respect is the end of the fragment where the *calf princess is* mentioned. The very expression *beef-princess* or *Chicago beef-princess* is quite significant. It turns out to be the bearer of obvious irony, but paradoxically, by referring to provincial soirees as *little tacky*, the writer is true to the flavor of elitism he is ironizing.

Both characterize F.S. Fitzgerald as a linguistic personality. The elitism of the linguistic personality is unambiguously manifested in the name of the *Chicago beef-princess*. The subtext is obvious. The writer is ironizing those who got rich by selling meat. In fact, of course, there is no cause for irony here. For example, we can remember that any rich Americans in Europe are no less ironic, including those whom F. S. Fitzgerald would hardly ironize. The same pattern of snobbery is revealed here. European snobbery towards Americans, albeit rather good-natured, is perfectly represented in A. Conan Doyle's The Hound of the Baskervilles.

By calling the Chicago meat kings cow kings or veal kings and their daughters veal princesses, the writer, on a completely unconscious narrative level, reveals himself as a representative of the families that made America. Regardless of their origins, these famous families can be considered the American aristocracy. F.S. Fitzgerald certainly belongs to such a family. This is the reason for the expression *Chicago beef-princess*. In any other situation, he would simply say that Chicago's wealthy tend to find provincial soirees somewhat tasteless.

Or, for example: "John T. Unger was on the eve of departure. Mrs. Unger, with maternal fatuity, packed his trunks full of linen suits and electric fans, and Mr. Unger presented his son with an asbestos pocket-book stuffed with money. "Remember, you are always welcome here," he said. "You can be sure, boy, that we'll keep the home fires burning." "I know," answered John huskily. "Don't forget who you are and where you come from," continued his father proudly, "and you can do nothing to harm you. You are an Unger - from Hades" (25, p. 5).

The motif of Hades-Hades-unbearable heat continues. The irony of the author ceases to be hidden, otherwise it is impossible to explain the suitcase full of electric fans. Against the background of electric fans, the linen suits look more harmless, since it is a change of clothes after all.

In itself, such persistence in emphasizing the expression associated with a single motif can be puzzling. However, F. S. Fitzgerald does not miss a single opportunity to emphasize the theme of "heat". It is clear that by unfolding this theme, he creates an integral semantic and stylistic paradigm characterized both by an appeal to mythological origins and by being loaded with local cultural and culturological background information.

The whole fragment is imbued with cultural Americanisms, which in Fitzgerald's speech unambiguously characterize him as a linguistic personality. From this point of view, the logocentrism of the text is obvious. Another thing is that it is rather difficult to distinguish here the author from the narrator. Let us only note that the concept "author" can correlate with such concepts as "writer", "storyteller", "narrator". Even the name of the writer - F. C. Fitzgerald - successfully fits into this row. As for the narrator, the narrator should rather be understood as a narrator who unconsciously presents a particular narrative of great importance to a given culture. The marked evaluations contained in the text may be consciously included in the text by the writer as characteristic and characterizing signs, but they may well be unconsciously narrative, giving away not so much the peculiarities of the characters as the writer himself as a linguistic personality.

One has to pay attention to all the details in the text, as none of them are accidental. If his mother stuffs his suitcases with linen suits, his father gives him a wallet full of money. Just a wallet full of money could not have functioned as a characterizing detail in the text. What matters is that it is stuffed. For an American's linguistic and cultural identity, the concept of "stuffed" becomes key. It may be an insignificant detail, but it takes on a special meaning in the context of our knowledge of American culture, where everything big - limousines, skyscrapers, people, smiles, etc. - is popular.

The farewell scene and the content of the dialog is just as playful. It is a purely American male dialog at parting. The father tells his son that he and his mother will keep the fire burning and that he will always be welcome at home. A somewhat strange conversation for a member of another culture between a father and son leaving home.

It is also important to pay attention to the father's admonition. No matter how small and provincial Gades might be, the father's message is that John must never forget who he is and where he comes from, must never tarnish himself with a dishonorable or bad deed.

Let's pay attention to another fragment: "So the old man and the young shook hands, and John walked away with tears streaming from his eyes. Ten minutes later he had passed outside the city limits and he stopped to glance back for the last time. Over the gates the old-fashioned Victorian motto seemed strangely attractive to him. His father had tried time and time again to have it changed to something with a little more push and verve about it, such as "Hades - Your Opportunity," or else a plain "Welcome" sign set over a hearty handshake pricked out in electric lights. The old motto was a little depressing, Mr. Unger had thought - but now" (25, pp. 5-6). A also: "So John took his look and then set his face resolutely toward his destination. And, as he turned away, the lights of Hades against the sky seemed full of a warm and passionate beauty" (25, p. 6) (25, c. 6).

When John and his father say goodbye, they shake hands, nothing more. However, on leaving the house John is in tears. This scene is remarkably reminiscent of an identical episode in I.A. Goncharov's novel Oblomov, when Stoltz leaves to study. As we remember, Stoltz's father only extends his hand to his son, whom he will not see for several years. Stoltz, though he is as German as his father, still grew up in Russia. He chokes on his tears, but holds back. I. A. Goncharov even allows himself to mock the reader, and by and large on the German character. The father called his son, the son thought, has awakened in him natural paternal feelings. In a hoarse voice he asks what his father needs, and he says that the horse's right cinch is loose. Stoltz replies that he will fix it on the way, now, he says, there is no time. But when he leaves the courtyard, he finds himself in the arms of the courtyard girls, who throw themselves at him with loud sobs. Stoltz can no longer hold back his tears, they are abundant streams flowing down his cheeks. He, too, cries loudly and kisses the courtiers.

John shows human emotion. He takes one last look at the city, and here we see a characteristic detail again. Above the gates of the city hangs a motto of the Victorian era. F.S.Fitzgerald does not cite the motto itself, but notes that this outdated motto seemed to him in this farewell moment extremely cute. John's father had shown a persistent desire to change the town motto from time to time. He wanted something like "Hades is your chance" to hang over the town. Although the old motto is not given, we realize that it is at odds with Father John's desire. As for his proposed motto, it is extremely characteristic of America. The key word and key concept in this context is the word *chance*. Here we see one subtle detail that characterizes not only and not so much Father John, but F. S. Fitzgerald himself and the American mentality. For Americans, the most important thing in life is to succeed. The most important concept for Americans of any age is the so-called *American dream*.

It is this string that F. S. Fitzgerald touches when he talks about Unger Senior's occasional attempts to change the town's motto. The context also suggests this reading, according to which Gades is not really an American town after all, if it retains its Victorian motto. If this is indeed the case, it becomes clear why the writer does not cite this Victorian motto. What becomes particularly important, however, is the motto proposed by John's father. If he wants to replace the old motto with a new one emphasizing that Hades is chance, therefore, the old one does not suggest the American dream.

Once again a demonstration of American character. John looks back, he is touched, even the old town motto seems quite sweet to him, he is glad his father was not able to change it, but in spite of his tears and emotion, he resolutely turns away from the town and heads off into the unknown distance.

In this context, the key word is *resolutely*. This word means "firmly", "unwavering", "resolute". It is clear that John is on his way to school, and no matter how hard it is for him, he will get there. He will not return home. However, *resolutely is* not just a constituent of the sentence, this word characterizes F.S. Fitzgerald himself as a linguistic personality. The point is that it is characteristic of Americans to break *unwaveringly* with the sweet past. The lovelier the past, the more unshakably they break with the past. There is another point worth noting. The discourse relevant to America and Americans indicates that there is a myth of American steadfastness in the minds of this nation. The same myth is compounded about the vigor of this nation, its fearlessness, its ability to work, etc. In other words, the ideologues of the nation have created and diligently maintain various myths that help them live and win. By ideologues one cannot understand only politicians or philosophers. For example, a great merit in the creation of this myth belongs to writers. Through the efforts of Jack London, Fenimore Cooper and even such a writer as E. Hemingway in the minds of not only Americans, but also the whole world created an image of a people not afraid of difficulties, overcoming everything and capable of anything. Thus, the word *resolutely* in the most ordinary sentence actualizes a significant amount of background information.

The word *destination is* also important in this sentence, but it is not as significant as *resolutely*. In addition, it is even somewhat ironic.

For a great master, which, of course, is F.S. Fitzgerald, a natural and maximally close to reality portrayal of reality is characteristic. That is why the steadfastness of the protagonist in this situation correlates with the charm of the lights of Gades against the background of the evening sky. The author of some modern American action movie would fixate on the said *steadfastness* and bring it to the mythologically maximum limit and thus to absurdity. F.S.Fitzgerald, on the other hand, reveals the spiritual world of the hero and his condition at that moment in parallel tones, making it clear that John is an ordinary favorite child from a wealthy family. This child is leaving his father's home for the first time, so he is touched. But this is not just any child, but an American child, which means that he is the bearer of special moral values, among which determination dominates. F. S. Fitzgerald here turns out to be the narrator of the folk epic about the American character, which forms an essential part of the narrative. In our opinion, the semantic and stylistic facts under consideration organize the syntagma not on a conscious, but rather on an unconscious level. F. S. Fitzgerald draws the image that is common for him. The point is not even that John or anyone else discovers these qualities. The point is that courage constitutes an ideal for him and for entire generations. Here the writer shows himself not only as a linguistic person, but a linguistic person who discovers his own moral content. The writer cannot go beyond his self-consciousness, nor, indeed, can anyone else. Thus, even in ordinary everyday sketches there is a high pathos of American self-consciousness. Creating the image of a teenager, the writer reveals himself as a linguistic and spiritual personality, a carrier of some energetic charge.

From the point of view of the peculiarities of linguistic personality, F.S. Fitzgerald's story may well be considered an encyclopedia of American life. In this respect, the writer's texts are still waiting for their researchers.

LIST OF REFERENCES USED

1. Bogin G.I. Acquiring the ability to understand: works of different years. Tver: Tver State University, 2009.

2. Vezhbitskaya A. Metatext in text // New in foreign linguistics. Issue VIII. Linguistics of text. Moscow: Progress, 1978.

3. Vejbicka A. Comparison of cultures through lexis and pragmatics. Moscow: Languages of Slavic Culture, 2001.

4. Wisson L. Russian problems in English speech. Words and phrases in the context of two cultures. Moscow: R. Valent, 2007.

5. Wittgenstein L. Tractatus Logico-Philosophicus // Philosophical Works. Part I. M.: Gnosis, 1994.

6. World Encyclopedia: Philosophy. M.: AST, Mn.: Harvest, Modern Literator, 2001.

7. Zvegintsev V.A. History of linguistics of XIX-XX centuries in essays and extracts. Part I. Moscow: Uchpedgiz, 1960.

8. Ermakova O.I. Ethics in computer jargon // Logical analysis of language. Languages of ethics. Moscow: Languages of Russian Culture, 2000.

9. Ivanova D.V. Features of speech behavior of Russians in the situation of overcoming the conflict (in contrast to Americans) / Problems of speech communication. Issue 11. Interuniversity collection of scientific works. ed. by M.A.Kormilitsyna. Saratov: Izd-v. Saratov University, 2011.

10. Karaulov Y.N. Russian language and linguistic personality. Moscow: Nauka, 1987.

11. Krasnykh V. Fundamentals of psycholinguistics and communication theory. Moscow: ITDGC "Gnosis", 2001.

12. Scientific Life. V International Conference on Cognitive Science // Voprosy Linguoznaniya, No. 3,2013.

13. Ozhegov S. I. Dictionary of the Russian language. Moscow: Russian language, 1990.

14. Pesce M. Content analysis and discourse theory // Quadrature of meaning. The French School of Discourse. M.: Progress.

15. Pushkin A. C. Complete Works in 10 Volumes. Volume 7. - L.: Nauka, 1978.

16. Rosenthal D.E. Practical stylistics of the Russian language. Moscow: Higher School, 1977.

17. Rozin V.M. Cultural Studies. M.: FORUM - INFRA-M, 1998.

18. Soper P.L. Fundamentals of the Art of Speech. Moscow: Yachtsman, 1995.

19. Sossur F. de. Works on linguistics. Moscow: Progress, 1977.

20. Fricke J.A. Linguistic personality of the author of the artistic text and idiostyle: the basis of linguopragmatic comprehension of phrase nomination - 2012. - [electronic resource] - http://superinf.ru/view_helpstud

21. Heidegger M. Being and Time. M.: AD MARGINEM, 1997.

22. Hemingway E. A short happiness of Francis Macomber // Hemingway E. Collected Works in 4 volumes. Volume 1.M.: Khud.lit., 1968.

23. Schimmel A. The World of Islamic Mysticism. Moscow: Aleteia, Enigma, 1999.

24. Hemingway E. The short happy life of Francis Macomber // Modern English and American short stories. M.: International Relations Institute Publishing House, 1961.

25. The stories of F. Scott Fitzgerald. NY: Charles Scribner's sons, 1954.

Buy your books fast and straightforward online - at one of world's fastest growing online book stores! Environmentally sound due to Print-on-Demand technologies.

Buy your books online at
www.morebooks.shop

Kaufen Sie Ihre Bücher schnell und unkompliziert online – auf einer der am schnellsten wachsenden Buchhandelsplattformen weltweit! Dank Print-On-Demand umwelt- und ressourcenschonend produzi ert.

Bücher schneller online kaufen
www.morebooks.shop

Printed by Books on Demand GmbH, Norderstedt / Germany